EARTH
in
ASCENSION

Nancy Anne Clark, Ph.D.

EARTH
in
ASCENSION

Nancy Anne Clark, Ph.D.

*This book is dedicated to all the awakening World Servers.
You are making a difference by simply being.*

Light Technology Publishing

Cover art by
Douglas Taylor

Cover design by
Faye Richards

ISBN 0-9648307-6-0
Published by
Violet Fire Publishing
P.O. Box 39051
Tucson, Arizona 85751

Printed by

MISSION
POSSIBLE
Commercial
Printing

P.O. Box 1495, Sedona, Arizona 86339

Acknowledgments

I would like to thank the following people who have made a difference in my life. The three greatest influences in my adult life have been Katusha, Andre and John, who made it possible for me to learn my lessons more quickly. S. Lucinda Hubing needs to be recognized as one of the advanced order of humans bringing about a change in how the church is viewed. The outstanding work of Profs. Marilyn and John Rossner opened wide the door to the world of the nineties through their international conferences. Simultaneously walking through the door were several wonderful people from the area then known as Czechoslovakia. They have become the very special "family" I now have in that area of the world and I shall be forever grateful. With deepest love I acknowledge my large Band of Angels in the Milwaukee area who kept me growing as fast as I could so the teacher might stay ahead of the students. Lastly, and most importantly, I give thanks to my Creator and my guides in spirit who have been by my side as long as I can remember, helping me to stay awake and on my path.

Other works
By Nancy Anne Clark, Ph.D.

Advanced Healing Techniques Video
Using BioGetic Holophasing
Healing the Past, Healing the Future

Meditation Audio Tape Series
entitled Journeys of Remembrance

Journey to Atlantis and Lemuria
Journey to Discover Your Angels
Journey to Access the Light Body

Call 1-800-795-TAPE
for a free catalog
For Seminar Information on
World Ascension
and
Advanced Healing with BioGetic Holophasing
or write:

Violet Fire Publishing
P.O. Box 39051
Tucson, AZ 85751

TABLE OF CONTENTS

PREFACE

The second half of the twentieth century has been unlike any other period in the millions of years of Earth's history. The souls of incoming babies were asked to declare their intentions, as were those already incarnated on the physical plane. They either agreed to work on their own journeys into the Light of the fifth dimension, thereby helping the planet, or they chose not to be a part of the Plan.

Those earlier decisions did not make any discernible difference until the 1980s when it became evident that the polarities were becoming more pronounced. Then the dark elements found it more difficult to hide in the shadows. The true purposes of individual and group actions became easier to discern. Humanity was transforming. It was the beginning of actual biological mutation. People have continued developing their minds and supersensory abilities. It has become increasingly difficult to con or take advantage of the growing population. This change always takes place on an individual basis before it reaches the collective.

As the end of the Twentieth Century rapidly approaches, the distinction between the two groups of humanity continues to widen. It is as if two men know they will be taking a trek high in the Himalaya Mountains. One has been working toward this exciting adventure for the past few years. He has been slowly changing his diet and exercising with regularity, while mentally and emotionally preparing himself for the upcoming challenge. The other man considers himself physically, mentally and emotionally fit. He has no intention of making any changes in his lifestyle, for he prefers the situation just as it is. When the day of the journey arrives, he will simply go. It is the way he has always operated and he sees no reason to change.

Immediately upon reaching their destination by helicopter at the 14,000-foot level, the two men react to their environment quite differently. The distance between the two becomes increasingly greater as they arduously climb higher and higher. The hiker who has conditioned himself over time makes daily progress, truly enjoying the adventure and yet awed by the new vistas that appear at every turn.

In contrast, the other man is not aware of the growing separation from his friend because of the misery he is experiencing. Every step forward brings greater physical pain. It seems every organ and muscle in his body is rebelling against what they are being asked to do. In addition to the physical suffering and inability to get sufficient oxygen, his mind is frustrated, and emotionally he is becoming increasingly depressed and angry. He might strike out at those around him and blame them for choosing too difficult a route. He even considers the possibility that the sherpas would carry him if he became too ill to walk. Or he could simply give up. If he should suddenly slip on loose pebbles and careen headlong into the valley below, all his pain and anguish would be ended. He would not have to think about why this was happening to him. His family and friends would only react to their tragic loss. He would be free.

This analogy is repeating itself in every sector of the world with each passing moment. On one hand, there are the Light-seekers. They may or may not be consciously aware of the coming Earth changes but they are trying to become better world citizens. They feel a certain responsibility to make the planet cleaner and safer for future generations. They sense a growing need to learn more about life after death, UFOs and angels. Each day more people around them are talking about synchronistic events and receiving prophetic dreams or hunches. These New Agers are frustrated by the portion of their tax dollars which is spent in research and yet the medical profession is no closer to curing nagging backaches, the common cold or birth defects. Increasing numbers of people are looking to alternatives, often ones that return them to a more natural way of living life.

It is interesting for their families and friends to see the changes in them and to note how they are planning for the future. Seekers on the path no longer blame their childhoods or upbringing for who they are today. Rather, they are grateful for the experiences, realizing how much those events contributed to their personal growth. This new humanity flows with life's challenges while observing the reactions of others. Each day brings a definite excitement as they realize they chose to be here at this momentous time. They are delighted to meet new friends whom they instantly feel they have known forever. From a childhood of thinking differently from the other kids, often not even resembling their biological families and feeling like strangers to life on Earth, New Agers are awakening to a greater awareness on many levels. Life, although still a challenge, is suddenly thrilling!

Quite the opposite is true of the soul who has made the inner decision to stay in the seeming security of the way things were. He is overwhelmed as his most carefully detailed plans are continually interrupted and changed or canceled. He feels tremendous loss over the number of people around him who have become seriously ill or are involved in unusual accidents. There is tremendous apprehension over thoughts of aging and death. The more life around him changes, the more this person clings to the past. These changes might include the loss of a job, a divorce, his "perfect" child suffering substance abuse, or the terminal illness and eventual death of a loved one. He believes he has lost all control of his life. And as he believes, so he creates his reality.

Each woman and man is the creator of his or her own destiny. He very carefully chooses the lessons he wishes to learn and then tests himself to make certain he has learned them. The exciting prospect is that by learning all those lessons and clearing so much past karma, he will never again have to go through this level of experience, never again need to return to a third-dimensional reality unless he chooses to do so. And most fantastic of all is the realization that he no longer needs to suffer illness, aging and death — *in this lifetime*. It is not some far-off reality; the time is *now*.

This book is an uplifting glance into Earth's past, present and future. There are many books on the Grays, the Reptilians and the Trilateral Commission. There are maps showing the destruction of the land masses due to earthquakes and the melting of the polar icecaps. Dozens of books now reveal the predictions of many seers, including Nostradamus and Edgar Cayce. Each author's story is a reflection of where that person was at the time of the writing. No future prediction expresses absolute truth or is one hundred percent accurate. Moment to moment, humans can and do change the future by the way they think, feel and act.

Several months ago, at four in the morning, I was given a glimpse into the future. It was a scene filled with such joy that it was difficult for the people in my vision to contain their excitement. The purpose of this writing is to share with the world the thrilling events that have already begun and continue to escalate. I am convinced that humans are approaching a time when they will be able to create their own scenarios of the probable future. Two people standing side by side will experience the same event from two entirely different perspectives. One will view an incident with uncertainty or fear while the other will be filled with joy and growing peace. Everyone chooses in each moment how he wishes to view life, and it is never too late to change perspectives. In fact, those recently aware of the New Age phenomenon accomplish in a few months what took many people years to attain, because the pattern is now established.

The teacher in me wishes to share all the information I have so that life might be easier for everyone in the months and years ahead. My greatest desire is that this message trigger a knowing that resides deep in the heart. For some, it will be the verification they are searching for, the great "Aha!" It has been extremely gratifying to hear people from many countries saying that the vague feeling they had been carrying with them for so long had finally been clarified.

Many blessings on the journey. Namaste!

INTRODUCTION

The roller coaster ride of this lifetime is getting more thrilling with each passing day. Circumstances whirl people into situations and "chance" encounters before they have caught their breath after the last learning adventure. Time is either dragging painfully slowly or rocketing by, creating the feeling that the moment has been lost. Time doesn't seem to possess the same continuity it used to have. There is the somewhat frightening phenomenon in which almost as quickly as a person thinks a thought, it becomes reality. At times, it is not what was expected on the physical level, but it is certainly the lesson that needed to be learned at that moment. Many people are going through feelings of elation, loss, bewilderment, excitement and are having unusual food cravings, especially for sweets. One day they feel like hibernating and retreating from the world, and the next day they are filled with energy. There are days when they can survive on just a few hours of sleep. The only certainty in life is that every aspect of it is now changing and uncertain.

The reason for these strange feelings will become clear to the reader as he or she journeys into the past to access the planet's little-known history. Next the reader will discover that Earth and everything on her surface is in the process of moving from the third dimension to the fifth, from the Age of Pisces to the Age of Aquarius. Most fascinating of all is the information now being revealed about the return to the physical realm of spiritual teachers, masters and guides in their great descension, which is to occur within the next few years. Humans will be able to see them and converse with them. They will demonstrate superior ways of living during the coming changes. Some of their harmonious methods and suggestions are revealed in the final chapters.

There will be a day like no other. It will begin with a certain restlessness, but other than that, nothing will seem out of the ordinary. Every man, woman and child will follow his or her usual routine. Then some of the population will develop a sense of urgency that will replace the restlessness. Many individuals who consider themselves to be on the path will be triggered. It is those who call themselves Lightworkers and New Agers, those who through meditation, spiritual practices and devotion to God who will suddenly feel compelled to stop whatever they are doing and go outside. From their places of business, their homes or their cars, these people will have the overwhelming urge to look up to the heavens. And as they do, these dedicated workers will see what will appear to be hundreds of parachutes filling the sky and slowly floating down. As they become clearer, they appear to be orbs, or geometries of light. The lights will become larger and larger. Finally, as they touch down on Earth, it will become evident that these visitors who have arrived in such a spectacular and miraculous way are radiant beings of Light. Who are they? Where have they come from, and why?

In an unparalleled event for any planet or star, humans will be receiving help from their elder, wiser galactic brothers and sisters as well as the angelic kingdom. Life would be difficult without their assistance. Now and during the coming years, enormous amounts of love are being showered on the planet. (That is why those on the path feel such an excitement with every new day that dawns.) This tremendous flood of love is rebuilding the connection between humans and other galactic beings that has been broken for nearly thirty thousand years.

Some people have heard that in a very short period of time, the known world will disappear. It is true that the third dimension and all its duality will cease to exist on this planet. Everything material will be of no real value. All the toys people have amassed will be useless. Not one item that depends on electricity or fossil fuels will operate. There will be no telephones, radios or televisions for communication.

Some people will feel temporarily cut off from the world just at a time when the planet seemed to be shrinking. More people than ever before are traveling to formerly inaccessible places. They can watch the evening news and see what is affecting other people on the opposite side of the world. What a tremendous shock it will be for those accustomed to personal power and control to find themselves without electronic equipment. They will feel they have lost everything worth living for. Governments will be in chaos. Business will cease as people concentrate their efforts on survival.

Others may find themselves in countries far from their loved ones because they had left home for business or pleasure. They will need to adjust in unfamiliar surroundings. As strange as it sounds, many will be in just the right place to be of great assistance to the local people. Everyone, at a higher level of his being, will choose the place he wishes to be as the dramatic events unfold. Most people realize by now that the shifting of the Earth's plates has already begun. The evidence is the increasing number of earthquakes of major proportions that have taken place over the past several years.

Many people who have spent this lifetime amassing fortunes and creating dynasties will not be able to bear the loss. These are the people who have not only built their worlds around material wealth but have also used their power for the subjugation of others. Such business magnates have lost touch with life beyond this third-dimensional reality. In their minds, nothing outside their world exists, so when there is no equipment to keep their corporations running, when their money and investments have no value, they will feel empty and alone and will think that life is no longer worth living.

During the period of days in which the most dramatic changes are occurring, many people will have little to do but review the meaning of their lives and decide what to do with their futures. For most of the population, it will be the first time in memory when there will be nothing to do and no place to go. There will be no sporting events, concerts, meetings, political rallies, performances and above all, no television or radio broadcasts. There will be minute upon minute, hour upon hour of silence – except for nature and, in the large cities, the cries and lamentations of bewildered humans.

What has been painted here is a grim picture of the coming changes, but it is only one possible scenario; there are many others. A great number of probable realities are filled with promise and with the hope, love and caring of millions of beings who are coming here in time to help all those who will accept their guidance.

Crime, poverty and destruction are creations of human negativity. They are not God's judgment upon people. The regions of the world that have experienced wars throughout all of history have a great need of cleansing. The Earth Mother has suffered every loss ever incurred in these areas. The time has come when she will take no more, like the mother whose naughty children have exhausted her patience. The inhabitants of those areas of tremendous negativity will create destruction by means of their thoughts and emotions as well as with their hands. It has already begun, as is evidenced by unseasonal storms and devastating floods in places where they have never occurred before. It is all part of the great cleansing and does not mean humanity has been abandoned.

Humans have felt very much alone in the universe, and with reason. For eons Earth has been isolated, quarantined from the rest of the galaxy. But it is important to understand that although humans have felt deserted, the truth is that Earth has always been watched over and loved by many who consider themselves to be the brothers and sisters of humans. They have never left and their vigilance never ceases, regardless of the troubles many humans have heaped upon themselves with their-greed and their need to be in control.

Growing numbers of the population are losing their need for power, as recent decades have shown. For the first time in United States history a war — the Vietnam war — was unpopular. Then, the 1960s ushered in attempts at communal living. There have been commitments by many national governments to health and economic cooperation between nations. People have rallied to send food and supplies to areas of natural disasters. Cultural exchange programs are helping people to understand the mores of others. Organizations such as the Peace Corps bring the expertise and experiences of various groups into contact with those who need better methods of agriculture, home building and hygiene. These endeavors reach across the lines of color, language and national boundaries. Little by little, an effort is being made to convey help and understanding to those less fortunate than others.

There are many who look at the broad picture of what is happening in the world, and instead of seeing positive changes, they focus on the wars that continue to be fought, the oppression of those in need, governments that are hiding the truth from citizens on the grounds that it would not be good for them, monopolies that control giant corporations and therefore the daily lives of millions, an educational system that certainly is not preparing young people for life in the next century, and religions that often cling to old fundamentalist dogmas and ancient rituals. They look at the problems of overpopulation, deforestation, pollution and the mountains of garbage piling up daily. By focusing on the problems that exist in every area of life, these people feel overwhelmed by the prospects for future generations.

There have always been those who look at the glass as being half empty rather than half full. On that basis, they continue to create their realities. It will soon be discovered just how people attract into their lives whatever they need. Over the past ten or twenty years, New Agers have been asking themselves to learn their lessons as quickly as possible. This is especially true of the young people, for they no longer have lifetimes to finish their work. Many on the path sense an urgency to complete their remaining tasks so that they are free to move forward with Earth into the fifth dimension.

Just how that will come to pass and the background information that follows is a guide to this time of great transformation. Every human, every living and nonliving thing is being affected. As Earth ascends, humans will be lovingly helped to move forward with her, if they so wish. It is the personal decision of each individual.

The Fall of Camelot

In the last days, God says, I will pour out my spirit on all the people. Your sons and daughters will prophesy, your young men will see visions, your old men will dream dreams. Even on my servants, both men and women, I will pour out my spirit in those days, and they will prophesy. I will show wonders in the heaven above and signs on the Earth below...before the coming of the great and glorious day of the Lord.

Acts 2:17-20,NIV

An event of unprecedented proportions is about to happen! It is so spectacular, so unbelievable that it will mystify everyone from top scientists, government officials and the religious hierarchy down to ordinary people in every sector of the world. This is the reason people chose to be here at this time. It is why many feel such a sense of urgency in their lives. They are about to participate in the end of an age and the end of Earth as she has always been known. With all the help Mother Earth, or Gaia, as she is often called, is receiving from other planetary entities, she is swiftly moving into the fifth dimension. Humans must also accelerate their vibrational frequencies to conform with the fifth dimension or it will be impossible to remain here. How can humanity change so dramatically in such a short time? Help is coming! Unparalleled blessings will be arriving from sky during a dramatic moment in history. To learn who they are and why they are coming, it is necessary to understand the events that have led up to this momentous occasion.

Earth is always changing. Every page that is turned on the calendar of history brings exciting new revelations regarding her adaptability and resilience. How wonderful it is to live here! Just as parents watch in amazement as their infant learns to smile, to communicate and to expand in consciousness, some people are now experiencing the same feelings about the planet, dimly recalling ancient visions of being with her since the beginning. Faintly stirring deep within are misty promises to stay with the Earth Mother until she could move into the Light. That Light is the vibrational frequency of the fifth dimension.

Not History but Herstory

This little planet called home has an interesting story. Earth is situated at the far edge of this universe, so to some it may seem relatively unimportant in contrast to the trillions of gigantic stars and planets that make up galaxies. But there is something unique about Earth, something so special that although she could have been abandoned on several occasions, some great being always stepped in to save her. It has been the deep belief of many, including those who are here now, that the Earth Mother is worth saving.

At one time Earth was a version of Camelot. The sun shone when the moon did not. The weather was always warm and tropical. There was never more than a few degrees variation in temperature from morning to night or from pole to pole. No snow could be found at the polar caps. (In the early 1800s, when the U.S. government funded an expedition to Antarctica, Admiral Byrd discovered pollen frozen in the snow.) Inhabitants had no concerns about earthquakes, typhoons, tornadoes or, in fact, storms of any kind, for they did not exist. If there was a noticeable wind, it was only a gentle breeze.

Such an incredible scenario was possible because Earth was protected by a bubble of misty energy that was composed of Infinite Light particles of Christed energy.[1] All planets, stars, suns, solar systems, galaxies and universes in harmony with Source are surrounded and protected by the Light of Creation. Beams entering a planet also align with Infinite Light, varying it according to the planet's polarity. This Light is directed out from the center of creation to all the suns which then step-down the energy to the necessary vibration of a particular planet. In addition to the Light of Creation and energy from her immediate sun, Gaia also receives beams in various colors and frequencies from the planets and constellations of the zodiac. All vibrational frequencies are constantly monitored so energy can be adjusted up or down as needed.

Grids and Pyramids

Every planet and heavenly body has a unique grid structure, or web. At particular intervals in the grid, great power points or energy vortexes are located. That critical balance of Light Energy is maintained in this solar system by pyramids and to a lesser extent by sacred circles and structures such as those at Stonehenge in England. These great monuments broadcast energy which then surrounds and penetrates landmasses and even other planets. Earth's stability has been maintained by major pyramid complexes strategically situated within a thirty-degree zone above and below the equator.[2]

It will be learned that the pyramids were built far earlier than is currently believed, and they were not built by Egyptian slaves but by highly evolved beings who would be termed extraterrestrials. If they had been built by slave labor, the feat certainly could be repeated at the present time, but modern technology cannot build equivalent structures, nor can the existing pyramids even be restored to their original specifications. Soon the world will know that the pyramids were certainly never built as monuments to pharaohs or as burial chambers. Primarily, they are receivers and transmitters located at crucial power vortexes. In addition, these unique energy centers were also the sites of formal ceremonies and initiations by the great masters.

In the Great Pyramid at Giza is a giant brain, or computer, that connects it to other pyramids by means of light projections. In the past these light energies were beamed not only to the other pyramids on Earth but also to centers for communication throughout the universe. The Great Pyramid of Cheops is also a time sensor, registering the current levels of human evolvement, and is situated on the seventh chakra of the planet.

Originally, the Great Pyramid was finished with a smooth white limestone surface that sparkled in the sunlight. The capstone was a pyramid on top of the pyramid and was constructed of crystal and gold; it was was capable of greatly amplifying light waves of information being sent or received. This crystal capstone also operated in a way that is somewhat similar to a modern nuclear accelerator: it could draw up the Earth energies into a dynamic vortex. That is why pyramids were powerful sites for initiation and human transformation.

The Great Pyramid of Cheops had several chambers that were used for the transmutation of energy. Along with the other pyramids at Giza, it was one of the main locations of mystery school teachings on Earth. There, the aspirant and the hierophant went through the levels and rites of initiation. The pyramid is connected to the Sphinx not only by a tunnel but also on higher vibrational levels. The Sphinx, with a human head and the body of a lion, is the symbol of man's future destiny. The lion symbolizes the sun; as people evolve, they will become radiant suns of the Godhead, space beings and beings of Light.

The familiar Bible story of Mary and Joseph fleeing with the baby Jesus to live in Egypt will take on a new meaning when humanity gains greater understanding. Mary and Joseph intentionally took Jesus to that sacred site in Egypt so that they could be physically near Jesus' future masters and teachers. Jesus became mentally, or telepathically, connected to them during his first two years. Once the connection was made, the masters could guide Jesus through thought transference during future years, regardless of where he was. It will be understood that Jesus was an adept, a master who later took his initiations in the pyramids also — but that is the subject of another book.

Arks and Ankhs

Twenty-first century humans will arrive at a new understanding about the Ark of the Covenant. There are various Biblical references to the Ark in Genesis, Numbers, Kings and Samuel. They provide several descriptions of the Ark as a coffin or a portable box or chest that might have held the two stone tablets bearing the law that was delivered by Moses. One definition, in *Harper's Bible Dictionary*, says the Ark was the "direct manifestation of God which could strike dead anyone who desecrated it." Several arks of the covenant existed at various sites on Earth, and they did appear as large boxes that could be transported on poles.

Arks were initially brought to Earth by humanity's ancestors from space to create the pyramids. An ark — or more specifically, the energy source within an ark — was capable of emitting several types of strong rays, depending upon the immediate purpose and requirements. This energy source was a generator/transformer capable of generating and storing alternating frequencies. A second function was to direct laser-like beams great distances. The force was so powerful that it could cause sudden death for those who did not know how to use it or did not wear protective clothing.

Several other tools were brought to Earth as well. Smaller energy transformers were used for projects requiring much less power. The majority of these smaller units were in the form of the familiar ankh.

Rather than being made entirely of metal, as they often are now, the ankhs used for directing energy had round wooden handles to prevent the user from being electrocuted. A small version of the ankh was frequently used for tuning and aligning the energies of the physical human body with its various subtle bodies.[3] Illness on physical, emotional, mental and spiritual levels could be healed instantly by realigning the electromagnetic frequencies of the various bodies. The familiar shape of the ankh has survived many eons, although, as with many other things, its original purpose has been forgotten. Today some people feel drawn to wear an ankh near the heart, as it helps them to feel calm, peaceful and balanced. Others wear them as protection against death, sensing fragments of the initial intent.

As indicated above, one of the purposes of the arks was to build pyramids at specific locations. That was accomplished by directing an energy beam at the granite mountains. The laser-like beam could precisely measure and cut the stone to the exact dimensions required. The rock substance in the path of the laser would vaporize, or change into an invisible higher vibration. Another frequency of the ray could neutralize the gravitational field surrounding the giant cut stone and then project the stone along a vibrational "path" between the mining area and the plateau at Giza or any other distant site.

Obviously, those who brought the arks to Earth and worked with them were not ordinary humans. They were the original builders and planners of this and many other solar systems. These space brothers and sisters were more god-like than human; they were much taller, stronger, more intelligent and more advanced in all ways. Their plans were to establish a world of harmony and cooperation among the animal, vegetable and mineral kingdoms on Earth, using humankind as the guardian of those kingdoms. Of course, all kingdoms were to be in complete accord with the sentient Mother Earth, herself a living spirit. Every pyramid was placed in the exact location necessary for balancing planetary energies deep within the Earth, on the surface and in the ethers above. They synchronized all the various planes of less density that interpenetrate the physical plane of matter.

Thousands of underground passages connect not only the Egyptian pyramids but also many other pyramids and holy structures around the world; and these passages even join great cities built within the Earth. Some of the tunnels have been destroyed by the shifting of Earth's tectonic plates but others remain, connecting sacred sites to one another.

The importance of the pyramidal shape throughout the universe will be understood when the language of sacred geometry is understood. It will be discovered that the very basis of the physical human being is composed of light pyramids. In fact, scientists observing blood crystals through electron microscopes are already aware of the blood's pyramidal shapes.[4]

Mariner 9 sent back to Earth pictures of pyramids on Mars, so there is proof they are not unique to this world. Pyramids of Light are the gateways to higher dimensions. They are capable of altering or coalescing time, space and matter so they meet the exact requirements for creation or evolution.

The major pyramids on Earth, and specifically the Great Pyramid at Giza, have lost most of their former capabilities for several reasons. The first is that when an ark was placed within a pyramid and both were located over a powerful Earth vortex, the resultant energy was like that of a large nuclear reactor. Now all the arks are missing — and with good reason. Humanity would surely have destroyed itself and the planet by now if the arks had been accessible.

A second reason the pyramids were so powerful then but no longer are is related to the high vibrations of the gods and goddesses, the masters and hierophants[5] who were often present in the various pyramid temples. They taught the ancient wisdom to those who were ready to learn it. Only those who had reached a certain vibrational frequency were allowed to enter, thus keeping the energy at the highest possible level. The effect of high frequencies works both ways; the average human becomes ill as a result of exposure to frequencies higher than his body is accustomed to tolerating. This effect has resulted in what is called "the curse of the mummies." Tombs that had been sealed throughout the centuries still contained the original high frequencies. When grave robbers with low negative vibrations entered those chambers, their hearts could not take the instant shift in vibration.

Many pyramids are crumbling to ruin at this time because Earth is being restructured. Her grid lines are changing. Many of the former sites no longer have the powerful energy they once had. New energy transceivers, transformers and stabilizers of etheric vibrations will be placed at proper locations as the new grids are established. Soon the people of Earth will learn once again the purpose of such structures. All humanity will be helped technologically in these matters by the arrival of their more advanced brothers and sisters.

Lastly, many pyramids have lost their high vibrational frequencies because of the attitudes and purposes of visitors over the centuries. The original intent has not been maintained. For thousands of years, robbery was the main motive for being in the pyramids. Pyramids also were sites of deliberate destruction and desecration by Christians who believed their Christian god was the only god. Intent creates an energy vibration, whether positive or negative. It is gratifying to know the mystery schools of the future will be attended by thousands of students having access to all the information that, in the past, has been available to only a select few.

Gods of Creation

What happened on Earth that resulted in the departure of all those highly evolved beings with advanced technologies? It is important to understand that each planet is an experiment in creation. There is no set pattern for a star, a solar system or a galaxy. Each planet is a chemical and mineral "soup." The various components of biochemical and astrochemical matter come together. Eventually, when planets are able to support life, they are seeded. Many beings or life forms from various galaxies participate in the project. Often there is cooperation among a number of galactic species to create a prototype, or root race, that can adapt to the specific surroundings. The purpose of genetically created beings is that they must be superior to other life forms on the planet but not superior in the sense of power. Rather, they should be survivors who will be caretakers of and caregivers to other evolving creatures, serving less developed species with loving compassion. Some species become strong and survive, while ninety-eight per cent weaken and will eventually die out.

This is Earth's story. Planetary neighbors such as Orion, Sirius, Arcturus and the Pleiades, together with many others, were involved in the creation of the life forms on this planet. Some of the visitors had the best of intentions, while others were motivated by selfishness and greed.

Humanity is just beginning to remember its history. Earth has been a place of great excitement from the very beginning because of the unusual plans for the planet. This entire solar system was created to be one of magnificence through diversity. Some species evolved over millions of years and then disappeared. Scientists keep moving back the age of Earth and revising the dates of the original appearance of humankind. That is good! But for many, scientific belief still revolves around the idea that all life forms have been evolving from the beginning, so they theorize that prehistoric beings could not possibly be as advanced as present-day civilizations. Soon it will be learned that since her creation, Earth has been home or a territory of exploration for many beings far more advanced than humanity is today. At times these civilizations were in harmony with each other. During some periods, great rivalries existed which resulted in tremendous wars and destruction due to attempts at domination by hostile beings.

When the true history of the planet is revealed in the near future, it will be learned that many of the myths and folklore that have survived to the present time have their foundations in truths that go back millions of years. These myths tell of giants and gods, of beings who were human and reptilian and half man, half beast. Stories have been handed down from parents to children, stories that told of the wind, the Earth and the Sun as powerful entities and of the gods and goddesses who tried to deal with them. All of these strange stories are much more fact than fiction.

Soon it will be understood that in the same way a human appears as a god to an ant, a rabbit or even a dog, there are huge elementals that make up an ocean or a giant redwood tree and even greater entities that actually embody the planets and stars. These elementals are the foundations of earth, water, air and fire. They also comprise the foundation of the human body. When this is understood, it becomes easy to conclude that the human body is composed of many smaller elemental beings. Everything is one and many at the same time.

Humanity learned from Einstein's theory that energy and mass are related to the speed of light. Mass, or matter, is denser energy because it vibrates at a lower frequency. At a subatomic level, everything reduces to energy, which is light. Scientists now believe subatomic particles are inseparable universal energy patterns. This means humans are linked to every other thing in the universe. This information expands the narrow opinion most people have of humans as God's crowning achievement.

The Creation Story

More and more people are beginning to believe that the Book of Genesis in the Bible describes two creations. Genesis 2:7 speaks of Adam's being created from the dust, clay or elements of the Earth. His creation was followed by that of plants and animals. If the information in the Bible is accepted as being accurate, what does it say about Darwin's theory of evolution? How could man evolve from apes when animals had not yet been created?[6] Later, woman was created. In Genesis 2:15-17, it says that humans were given subservient work as servants of God.

In contrast, there is the reference found in Genesis 1:26-27 (KJV): "And God said, Let us make man in our image, after our likeness; and let him have dominion over the fish of the sea and over the fowl of the air and over the cattle and over all the earth. . . ." It is important to note that God did not say, "Let me make man in *my* image . . . after *my* likeness." In both the King James version and the Hebrew version of the Old Testament, "elohim" translates as "gods" (with a small "g" rather than "God" with a capital "G"). That has been interpreted to mean that Jehovah represents God as guardian of the people and the object of their worship, while the elohim represent creator gods and controllers of nature. Recent researchers and authors also suggest that Jehovah is one of the elohim.

The second creation story (Genesis 6:1-4) informs the reader that "the sons of God went to the daughters of men and had children by them." This coupling obviously resulted in superior beings, which would refer back to chapter 1, verses 26-28 in which humans were made rulers over lesser creation. In this passage, it says that woman was created simultaneously with man. From this information, it appears there was an evolving human who was probably quite inferior in development as compared to the children that resulted from the union of gods and humans. Superior beings who could visit Earth in their spaceships would certainly be looked upon as gods when contrasted with those early humans who had developed relatively few skills and had only limited language.

Many books are currently available on this subject and some are listed in the reference guide. It is not the intent of the author to dispute any of the many viewpoints regarding Earth's ancient history. Each writer is coming from the perspective of his or her own inner guidance and past experience. None is invalid. Humans always base the interpretations of what they see, hear or intuit on their past conditioning, combined with their present level of spiritual maturity. They formulate opinions in the same way ten witnesses of an accident give ten differing accounts.

The original intention of the creator gods was that all humans would be biologically designed to be god-like, or gods-in-the-making. However, outside forces have had other plans for humans over the ages. These beings had alternative, or take-over plans that opposed the original purpose for Earth and of the creator gods. The aggressors wanted all experimentation to be under their direction, and their strategy was to deceive other planetary beings into bending to their will. These misguided, self-serving beings wanted humans to develop a consciousness that was limited so they could have control over humanity. To a great extent, their plan has been successful over the past twenty thousand years or so. Those spacebeings who wished to control the population have succeeded largely by keeping humans struggling for survival and in fear of the future. But that was not always the way it was.

There have been civilizations that have risen to the level of great achievements. Those people were capable of such wonders that present-day humans cannot conceive of equaling them. Early Earth residents, the sons and daughters of the space gods, could not only travel around the world with or without their ships, but they could also travel inside Earth to visit the beings who live there in cities that exist to this day. Their vehicles were able to change vibrational frequency to accommodate or penetrate the varying densities of matter. Spacecraft were used for short trips and even for intergalactic travel back to their planets of origin. (What a wonderful prospect for the many people today who are lonely for the planet they call home.) What ended much of that travel was that Earth's vibration was becoming increasingly dense and so were the frequencies of the higher beings. A time came when advanced beings simply could not come and go as they had originally.

Appearance and Apparel

The early god-humans were created in the image of their gods, and this is their present appearance. The most obvious exception was size, as many were eight or nine feet tall or even taller. They did not age or die throughout their many years on Earth, they only grew in perfection. These first truly great beings suffered no mental, emotional or physical illnesses or other problems associated with life in the twentieth century. Their clothing was fashioned from the rays and energies of light which were fused into natural products that amplified vibrations according to the owner's particular field of interest or position. Therefore, it was easy to identify the role of the individual by the color and style of his or her garment. Early god-humans knew which complementary mineral or gem to wear to enhance the vibration of their clothing's color. During special festivals and important occasions, they wore the robes of their particular order and used minerals for decoration.

Harmonious Living

Most of the population lived in cities of Light. The inhabitants worked for the good of everyone and everything. They recognized their oneness with all creation and were continuously aware of the laws of harmony, peace, joy and love. Everything they did was in accordance with universal law. They recognized their roles as guardians of Earth. A symbol of that role is found in the story of Adam and Eve in the Garden of Eden: God gave them "dominion" over every living thing, but it was never intended that having dominion would be interpreted as having power over anyone or anything. Humanity was meant to be protector and caretaker of Earth and everything dwelling in, on and above her.

Diet

The early humans ate mainly fruits and nuts from the trees plus some grains, and they ate a very small quantity compared to the amount of food humans eat today. (Scientists have long recognized that humans are not designed to be meat-eaters, as evidenced by the size and shape of their teeth and, more importantly, by their digestive systems. Animals who are meat-eaters have very short intestinal tracks to quickly eliminate waste. It is now known that meat from one meal remains in human intestines up to nine months before it can be broken down sufficiently to be released. Vegetarians of the animal kingdom have longer intestines to allow for the breaking down of food and the absorption of the necessary nutrients.) Consuming food was done more in celebration than for reasons of survival. Therefore, there was always joy in eating and drinking.

Relationships and Sex

Relationships were very different from those that exist today. Partners were chosen according to individual vibrational signatures. There was a specific range within which the two prospective partners' vibrations had to fall to be in harmony or in resonance with one another. This method automatically determined whether two people had the same interests and goals and were at comparable levels of spiritual evolvement.

In the beginning, sexual union was always expressed at the heart level, that is, at the fourth-dimensional level or above. Under those circumstances, the energies generated were transformed downward into the lower chakras for processing on the physical, emotional and mental levels and upward into the higher chakras, or spiritual levels. One of the purposes of sex was to attain or maintain a higher vibration, which is possible when both partners work toward the same goal. The intent was to remember the spiritual experience of ecstasy. The sexual experience was never practiced by putting attention on the physical, or first chakra level, or with any thought of domination over another, relieving stress or achieving personal gratification. The main objective of union was to become a more complete and whole being by reuniting the female and male aspects of self. Physical sex was performed much less frequently than it is today, and the *only* time it resulted in pregnancy was when the partners very carefully chose the exact time for bringing a new spirit into the physical realm. That is to say, no measures had to be taken to prevent pregnancy. It simply could not happen unless creation of a physical being was the intent.

Children

All children were awake to their divine natures. They were born fully conscious and aware of their purpose for choosing Earthly embodiment. Children were revered by all. Everyone was part of the extended family, so children never experienced feeling unloved or lonely. Nothing was withheld from them, so they grew in full knowledge of all the potential this realm held for them.

The Fall

All life was advancing. The Earth Mother and her experiment to allow beings from many places in the universe to procreate with various species on the planet continued working well for eons. Then the situation began to shift. There were those among the creator gods who preferred to keep humans at the level of automatons and slaves. They nearly succeeded by means of altering the genetic code. After some of the original RNA/DNA strands had been modified, humanity had little left with which to work.

The first great experience after losing a portion of the original DNA was the feeling of separation. Suddenly humanity no longer realized its connection to Source. People forgot their divine heritage. Grief, fear, loneliness and worry led to illness, aging and death. The human connection to the collective unconscious began to work to their detriment; each negative person served to hold the others down. Fear gradually permeated their subconscious minds, and humanity started to believe there would not be enough food, clothing and shelter for everyone to survive.

A growing mistrust opened the way to even greater suspicion and worry. Humans developed the need to have power over anything or anyone more vulnerable than themselves. This mistaken belief in their reasoning process led to ownership. Then the struggle to amass material goods began. Animals, land and even other people became property.

At the same time humans learned to judge both themselves and others. Of course they were more critical of themselves than of anyone else. Humans could never measure up to the standards they held in the recesses of their minds (subconscious memories imprinted in the RNA/DNA) from earlier periods of history. They judged themselves as being unworthy of God's love. When they did that, they became even further separated from their divine selves and from Source. This process describes "the fall"; humans fell out of the certainty that they were connected to one another and to the Supreme Creator.

That led to one dark age after another, and those negative beings who were trying to control humanity continued to create havoc from time to time. They attempted to destroy pockets of god-humans by using technologies such as the rays from the confiscated arks to exterminate the last of the colonies. That was the cause of the pole shift and the ensuing floods. The greatest upheaval threw Earth out of alignment with her galactic sun. Those undesirable beings have also been responsible for pandemics throughout history. Their terrorist tactics have induced even greater fear in the population.

Planetary Ascension

But Earth is coming of age! Great changes are taking place in every aspect of the world as humans have come to know it. Earth's transformation will affect not only the solar system but the entire galaxy. For millions of years there have been struggles and battles, and not just on this little planet; the problems extended far out into space. There have been renegades, outcasts, marauders and peacekeepers, just as the science fiction books and movies have portrayed. Sci-fi authors who see these vivid scenarios as pictures in their heads are tapping into what you might know as the Akashic Records.[7] As much as many humans would like to believe that existence beyond this planet is peaceful, it will become clear that similar difficulties exist in areas far removed from this remote corner of the universe.

For millions of years the Earth Mother has struggled for survival. There were times when the Galactic Council thought it might be better to leave this world to its own schemes, which would have resulted eventually in total annihilation of Earth. Many times there were opportunities for intervention. However, Earth and the Planetary Council had agreed to carry out an experiment in free will, and that would not be changed. Throughout time, there have been wars of control and manipulation. Yet in spite of all Earth's problems, there were those who dearly loved this little planet. They, like the Lightworkers here now, had vowed to stay with the world until her vibration could be raised beyond the vibration of those who perpetuated violence. This is now happening. After eons of being trapped in third-dimensionality, Earth and this solar system are finally moving into the higher dimensions.

This is affecting millions of individuals who are beginning to awaken. It does not matter where they live. People in huge metropolitan cities and in remote farm communities are experiencing a vague but deepening sense of urgency. Often there is no tangible reason for this shift in consciousness, but it is being noticed and talked about and even sung about. This new awareness is affecting people on an individual basis.

NOTES

1. Christ energy is the prana, chi, or life and Light force that permeates the universe.

2. Mas Toth. *Pyramid Prophecies.* Rochester, VT: Destiny Books, 1988.

3. Subtle bodies refers to the lower bodies: the etheric, astral (emotional) and mental.

4. J. J. Hurtak. *The Keys of Enoch*. Alhambra, CA: Sinclair Printing Company, 1987. p.38.

5. Hierophants were teachers in the mystery schools.

6. Human arms have never been structured for walking: they have always been used for tool-making. Feet are designed quite simply compared to those of many animals whose structures have become highly specialized, such as the horse, for example. The coccyx or base of the human spine has never been extended in a tail. Even the jaw is uniquely human. ". . . our human forms have existed in the Eternity as ethereal prototypes. . . ." according to Madam H. P. Blavatsky as stated in *The Secret Doctrine*. Kila: Kessinger Publications.

7. The Akashic Records contain all that has ever occurred and are available by accessing higher planes.

Awakening the Individual

So you and I are the problem and not the world because the world is a projection of ourselves, and to understand the world we must understand ourselves. Self knowledge is the beginning of wisdom and therefore the beginning of transformation and regeneration.

Krishnamurti

Not very long ago it seemed the world was filled with skeptics who went around complaining that "humanity will never change." Individuals lamented that if, indeed, anything were changing, it certainly seemed to be "for the worse." But now a growing number of people from every country are awakening to change . . . and the changes are indeed positive!

All awakening originates from a redefining of relationships. The examination of a one-celled protozoan would reveal that its reaction to the surrounding world causes action within the cell. The same description applies to the physical origin of a human as a fertilized egg. It reacts to the embryonic fluid in its mother's uterus from the very beginning of its existence. As it grows, its organs and glands all respond to one another to ensure survival of the organism. The cells are in constant communication with one another, according to research in Biocommunication by Robert Pressman.

Obstetricians, pediatricians and nurses have observed how newborns tune into those around them and immediately after birth begin to react in different ways to each person; so infants immediately set about creating relationships with others. Doctors say that by the age of nine months, babies have every person in their immediate surroundings figured out. Infants whose parents are deaf cease crying after several months because they have realized it does not garner a response. Babies already know what it takes to survive because it is encoded in their genes. As they expand in their discovery process, children continuously adjust their interactions with others, their personal identities and their growing consciousnesses. These adjustments occur on a subconscious level in children, but in adulthood they are often made because of a personal awakening or self-discovery.

There are exciting changes taking place among humans, not only in relationships but also in other areas such as spirituality and consciousness, and even in eating and exercise habits. These changes are occurring because many people are now coming into spiritual maturity. They are matriculating from their former need to control others and, quite conversely, are moving into a place where they are filled with the need to serve humanity.

Changing Identities and Consciousness

So many people, as they were growing up, heard expressions that went something like this:

"Children are to be seen and not heard."

"Mind your parents."

"Don't ask why. Just do it because I'm telling you to do it."

"I'm older so I know better than you."

For many centuries who a person became was based on his or her parents, grandparents, father's profession, family's social status in the community, education (or lack thereof) and what church was attended. It was expected that everyone would obey the rules and become what his or her parents demanded. Very few people were able to break that pattern and try to learn who they were as individuals. Most were content to be extensions of those who acted as their role models.

The most noticeable changes in this way of thinking began to occur during the sixties. Young adults rebelled against everything their parents stood for. They became aware of the pretense and hypocrisy that permeated almost every aspect of adult life. Budding Aquarians felt the injustice of war, and some were unwilling to die for a cause they did not believe in. Many refused to climb the corporate ladder. They expressed their rebellion and newly discovered freedoms by wearing colorful clothing, smoking pot, hitchhiking across the country or joining the Harley crowd. It was not long before they began to stay away from organized religion. The hippies were critical of government and most other established institutions. Young women began to speak out against the obvious gender bias that existed everywhere.

So many problems were exposed in a single decade that it will take many years to resolve the issues. Young Aquarians realized that situations that had been accepted for centuries could not be changed overnight, but they were the pioneers who set in motion the wheels that are now rolling toward the monumental Earth changes that are occurring. Their theme was, "Make love, not war." The flower children expressed a joyous innocence that spread from San Francisco around the world. They tried meditating, altered states of consciousness and communal living.

Hippies abandoned big business in America (as well as in other countries) and the struggle for material wealth. They could see what greed was doing to their parents and grandparents and wanted no part of it. These young adults looked with disillusionment at governmental decisions: against the background of the wisdom of the founding fathers, those decisions were found wanting. All the actions of the hippies made the rest of the population look at themselves a little more realistically. Rebellion against authority reflected their changing consciousness and identity.

Twenty years later, the children of the hippies were able to continue the changes begun earlier by their parents. The young people of the eighties were a little wiser and not as radical. Often these children had been raised with extended families. They were concerned about ecology, organic food and world peace. What great changes have come about in a very short period of time!

Changing Relationships

One of the most dramatic changes in the world over the past thirty-five years has been in the area of personal relationships, and that is where there is the greatest need. The old model for relationships was based on ownership.[1] Children and spouses, in particular, have been objects to be controlled. Relationships have existed in that form for thousands of years, and it is only now that humanity is discovering the shockingly high incidence of abuse on the part of both men and women.

Wives have belonged to their husbands and children to their parents throughout recorded history. Control always leads to abusive behaviors. Now that such actions are more difficult to hide (in the West), a new, freer, more balanced association can be established. This affects not only partnerships but also the relationship of parents to children and of parents to their parents. Couples are understanding they are valued partners when they can share equally. This is especially important when it comes to decision-making.

The decade of the eighties brought with it the idea of "househusbands." Some women are happy to be the breadwinners, exchanging roles with their partners. It is evident that there are women who are better at handling finances, while some men prefer domestic duties and raising children. The basis for a growing partnership is trust as well as love. Both individuals must be willing to give mental and emotional support and know *how* to receive it. Great joy occurs when both partners are growing at the same rate. It seems people are choosing partners for different reasons in the nineties than they did in the past.

The second area of relationships involves parents and children. Today, young people are becoming free to develop their potential rather than becoming all that the controlling person was not. They are being allowed to help make decisions that affect them personally, such as what school they wish to attend and where the family should go on vacation. Helping to make family decisions enables children to build confidence and to make wiser choices in the future. New Age parents are giving their children responsibilities involving enjoyable tasks as well as work-oriented duties.

It is important to realize that most children born in the past twenty-five years are far more advanced than their parents and grandparents were. Many are coming in with both hemispheres of the brain in balance. So these special beings are not as limited or narrow in their world views as their parents were. They have the ability to see a broader perspective. Some of these special humans are coming into this embodiment fully conscious, remembering past lives as well as their connection to everything.

The third area of relationships is a fairly recent phenomenon; it deals with the dependent relationship between adults and their elderly parents. Much has been written over the past several years regarding the role reversal that comes about when an elderly parent ceases to be a responsible adult and becomes like a child, requiring attention and care. This was not a problem several generations ago when people often did not live much beyond forty years. In addition to living longer, a large majority are now dying with multiple ailments or as a result of long-term illnesses, which creates a terrible strain on the family. In the future, it will be necessary to work on the causes leading up to this problem.

Humans are evolving into higher consciousness, which often allows an individual to recall his or her decision to come to Earth at this time to learn some of the many lessons available here. With this acknowledgment comes the understanding that there are no victims. It is never necessary to point an accusing finger or try to determine who should take the blame, for the truth is that whatever a person attracts into his experience is designed for his future growth. The challenge is to discover the reason for a particular lesson after difficult events have occurred. Viewing life as a series of lessons allows for rapid and far less painful growth. It is impossible to grow spiritually while feeling like a victim. Joy increases when it is understood that every circumstance in life has been chosen because it will facilitate the most rapid progress possible.

The last area of importance involves the need to be in relationships with like-minded people. The intention of new groups is to enjoy the best of one another, to share information, to meditate, chant or pray and to move into the highest energy circles possible. A visitor to such gatherings will definitely see a lot more laughing, hugging and sharing than at an ordinary meeting. There will be a noticeable absence of bad jokes involving judgment, sarcasm, racial slurs or gossip. Much of the energy of the individual participants is directed toward supporting one another.

Normally, a feeling of joy and optimism carries over into the way New Agers view daily living. They get trapped in the emotions of others less often. Instead, they allow friends and family to experience what is necessary for their growth. These people try not to be judgmental and yet continue to be supportive and loving without forming opinions.

As a group, they are less concerned about their retirement than other people. Most are looking forward to working in their true vocation, the one they came to Earth to perform. Many do not know exactly what that will be but they are not languishing because of the unknowing. They wait, somewhat impatiently at times, until whatever they are to do reveals itself. For the most part, these individuals possess greater patience than most other people as a result of their efforts to steadily increase their inner peace and harmony.

New Agers try not to place personal limits on the outcome of any future event or situation; "all this and more" is understood. They are open to the synchronicities of life. These spiritually advanced souls are in the habit of putting out a request to the universe and waiting for the gift to manifest. If the timing is right and if it is in the best interest of the individual and all others concerned, the request will *always* come to fruition. These people are discovering many natural laws that exist in the universe but have been forgotten by most of humanity. They are learning to manifest money, travel, perfect health and the right people, thus shaping their lives consciously. Every day becomes an experiment with newly discovered talents. They experience a great feeling of accomplishment when they manipulate time to suit the circumstance rather than "knowing" they will be late for an appointment.

The fundamental belief of New Agers is that Earth and everything on her is changing. That makes it an exciting time to be here and to be a part of these changes. Many New Agers felt very alone as children. Often they did not relate to family or friends or school. Many of them say they thought they had been adopted; that is how different they are from their biological families.

Many remember looking up to the heavens with the certain knowledge that the stars were their true home, and it was only in maintaining the connection that they felt a sense of belonging. It was an accurate perception, because many of these people had completed most of their karmic obligations[2] and therefore did not need to be born into family situations to work through relationship problems from the past. Instead, they chose the most advantageous birth circumstances, ones that would put them in the right places at the right times. They chose parents who would provide them with the situations to accomplish what they came here to do. Many New Agers were miserable for years, but that is what kept them awake as to who they were and aware that they had a mission to perform in this lifetime.

During the past ten years or so, many of these individuals have discovered friends whom they have immediately recognized as members of their celestial family. How exciting it is to meet someone for the first time and feel such an intense belonging! It is a feeling that reaches far deeper than physical love. No longer does it take months or years to get close to these "new" friends. They both simply continue where they had left off the last time they were together, whether that was on another planet or in another dimension. Many people are in transit, but that does not matter. At a recent gathering, everyone shared with the group why he or she had moved to this location, Tucson, Arizona. Nearly all said spirit had guided them here, and the majority had lived here for less than a year. People are relocating to areas they have chosen for the period of world changes. Once situated, they are meeting all those individuals necessary for loving support.

It has been said that the nineties is the time when many people will meet their true partners, and most commonly it will be the first time they have been together on this plane. In previous times, one of the partners has been here while the other was helping from another dimension. When it was time for the other to incarnate, the first partner was guiding from higher realms. What joy it is for some of these souls to be here together! Often, however, it can be the cause of great stress. Normally, people choose partners who are opposites in various ways so that when one is emotionally down, the other can be supportive. In these new relationships, couples are extremely sensitive because their vibrations are so closely aligned. Thus, when one is sad, it is difficult for the partner not to become dejected also. But life is fantastic when they are both up! When they understand this situation, they can accomplish miracles.

With such a strongly bonded partnership, they are able to work together for common goals and for the good of all humankind. Life is definitely easier when two people share compatible interests, thoughts and visions of the future.

Changing Youth

Young people equate coordinated clothing, tidiness and a well-groomed appearance with the obsession for material goods and status they see evidenced in their parents' behavior. They know too well the passion for amassing more and more consumer products that has been the motivating force for their parents and grandparents. They want no part of it. Children have chosen to be here at this time to change the old paradigm. Sometimes their unconscious mission is so overwhelming that they go too far in their efforts to rebel against the way things are. But for the most part, their rebellion is justified. Teens are responding to their souls' purposes without realizing it.

The sense of oneness felt by many young people is fascinating to observe. If a classmate is injured or dies, they all grieve, regardless of whether or not they had met the individual. Caring for those in trouble runs deep within them. Many young people do not seem to be inheriting their parents' prejudices as children have in the past. Most frequently, the color of a friend's skin does not matter. If a parent or relative points it out, the kids will make excuses to justify the friendship or relationship.

It is true that some teenagers around the world give the appearance of not caring about anything or anyone. Their actions demonstrate a backlash of anger and hatred, but it is actually fear. The deep feelings of frustration continue to escalate because those teens have never been shown any real purpose for living. Gang members in big cities do not have any sense of future. They have seen so many other kids die that each is convinced he will be next; existence is based solely on survival.

In addition to believing the future is nonexistent for them, they also are frustrated by an educational system that is hopelessly outdated. It is one that fosters superiority and rewards those with the greatest ability to memorize, a left-brained activity, ignoring those who are creative or right brained. Teens observe their unhappy parents telling them what to do, and it simply does not make sense to them.

Sociologists and psychologists are observing that a religious background certainly does not seem to help today's young people unless the leadership and the congregation are active, creative and forward-thinking. Youngsters usually rebel against any form of fundamentalist dogma. Children who have attended church regularly for years because their parents have insisted on it eventually object to what they perceive as limited, artificial rules. Again, young people today have developed a greater sense of observation than those in the past. They do not perceive their parents' lives as being happier, healthier or easier because they attended church for many years.

These observations about life around them do not make many of them bitter and alienated from society. More and more frequently there is news about the wonderful, creative ways some kids are helping others. Newspapers and television are reporting higher incidences of heroic deeds carried out by teens. Some kids are unselfishly giving what they can of their time and money to help those who cannot help themselves. They are forming groups and committees with their peers to carry out projects on a worldwide scale. They are interested in problems of global concern, such as pollution, and are very willing to help in any way they can.

Their willingness to help is becoming more evident in their relationships and partnerships. This is especially noticeable among young fathers who are trying to take a more active role in raising their children. With mothers working, young fathers are more likely than their fathers were to help with housekeeping chores. Many young people exhibit an increased capacity for understanding human nature at a very early age. Not being as left-brained or analytical as their parents, they are much more intuitive and sensitive to their surroundings.

All of the above characteristics are not the result of the influence of a particular religion, doctrine or education but rather are evidence of a greater sense of the spirit that exists in everyone. The young ones are beginning to exhibit the qualities of the sixth great root race. It has been said that the little children will lead the way, and they certainly seem to be starting.

Changes in Eating Habits

People in many parts of the Western world are becoming more health-conscious, which has led to a greater awareness of the body. Some individuals are experiencing deterioration or illness as the result of years of eating junk food or because of living in areas where the food supply is contaminated by pollution and pesticides. How sad it is to be in ill health at forty or fifty years of age when it is likely a person could be or should be living another thirty or forty years. Quality of life has become an obvious concern now that the population is living longer. It is no wonder that people are beginning to rethink their diet, and the amounts of fat, cholesterol and sugar they are consuming.

Twenty years ago many people believed a vegetarian diet to be unhealthy. After thirty years of research, it is now apparent that vegetarians have lower disease rates, greater stamina and longevity plus a marked increase in the quality of life they experience in their later years. The demands of increasing numbers of vegetarians have led large grocery store chains to carry organic produce. Many restaurants now include vegetarian meals on their menus, while pure vegetarian restaurants are opening to keep up with the growing demand. Groups of vegetarians are meeting regularly in many major cities, as they feel the need to support one another.

It is important to understand that people do not or should not become vegetarians overnight. Most vegetarians have the same story. They stop eating the most dense animal products first — bacon, hot dogs, sausages, steaks. It is customary to eat smaller amounts of red meat before cutting it out all together. After eliminating red meat from their diets, they stopped eating white meats, then poultry and finally fish. Often, the change to a vegetarian diet is founded on empathy for nature. Eventually, even the thought of eating a once-living, intelligent animal becomes incomprehensible. As Earth moves into the Aquarian Age, more people are becoming sensitive to animals' needs and rights. An often-used model is, "If it can run, crawl, fly or try to swim away from you, don't eat it."

Usually vegetarians will tell you that after a time of not eating a certain product, the delicious smell of hot dogs grilling or bacon sizzling in a pan will conjure up old memories. The mouthwatering experience can lead to sampling some previously enjoyed food, but unfortunately, the present taste is never as good as the memory. If a normal portion is eaten, the person's entire digestive system frequently rebels, as it is no longer accustomed to the lower dense vibrations, hormones and adrenaline found in such products. These denser substances remain in the system much longer than lighter fare and the person feels sluggish during that period of time. Meat-eaters normally carry between four and twelve pounds of undigested meat in their intestines. A hamburger stays in the body for six months to a year.[3] That accounts for the feeling of heaviness which vegetarians no longer experience.

Once the body is accustomed to operating on food that is of a higher vibration, an adjustment period is required when denser foods are eaten. One of the easiest ways to identify a negative reaction to food is by the amount of sleep required to process the food. For example, a typical response to overeating during the holiday season is the desire to lie down and take a nap after the Christmas feast. Recently I spent a month in Nepal. Although I did not eat meat, the food was much heavier than the food I was accustomed to, and even desserts were fried in yak butter. I was shocked to discover that my body required twelve hours of sleep a night rather than the customary four or five.

Often, today's Aquarian children prefer not to eat meat and poultry when given a choice. As they reach their preteen years, they frequently succumb to peer pressure and eat Big Macs. In spite of harassment and teasing, more and more teens are becoming primarily vegetarians. They are becoming very sensitive to the needs of all living things.

SUGGESTION

One method for determining what the body requires at any given moment is to select food according to color. Let your intuition tell you which would be the best choice: a yellow banana, a red apple, green grapes, oranges or food of some other color.

Your body needs living color to survive, so what does that tell you about French fries, potato chips and hot dogs? Dead food is not as good for you as living food. Most junk food is colorless but has had dyes added to give it greater appeal. That is also the reason manufacturers add both sugar and salt to the same products. It is one way they ensure that you cannot eat just one.

In the West many people had their own garden plots until the end of World War II. They gathered produce from their gardens just before meals, which ensured freshness plus a high vitamin and mineral content. People seldom added pesticides to growing crops. Farm animals were also fed living food, and as a result they were much healthier than they are today. Now boiled mash is the staple diet for poultry and pigs, but that weakens their systems, which leads to viral infections. To counteract the infections, animals are given massive doses of antibiotics. The end result is that the bacteria affect the quality of the food these animals become.

Another serious problem has surfaced as a result of eating meat and poultry products. Several studies of children have identified many problems resulting from high concentrations of synthetic hormones which are added to animal feed. One problem with serious consequences is that menarche, the onset of menstruation, is now common in girls eight years old. Rape of females by males under the age of ten was unheard of fifty years ago, but it has now reached epidemic levels.[4]

A study was done in Puerto Rico, where the population consumes large amounts of fast foods such as hamburgers and chicken. There five-year-old children are developing breasts and pubic hair, both boys and girls. The increased use of hormones since World War II has also caused our children to be taller.

Many people are becoming affected by the large amounts of adrenaline found in all slaughtered animals. Just before the moment of death, a surge of adrenaline rushes throughout the animal's body. Human bodies use adrenaline for the flight-or-fight response and it provides a massive burst of energy when that is needed. However, it is fatiguing and damaging to the body when adrenaline levels remain continuously elevated, and in addition, studies indicate that people become more aggressive, irritable and edgy.

It seems apparent that eating large quantities of meat produces too many side effects to ignore. For some years doctors have been recommending that Americans eat less altogether and include more vegetables and fruits in their diets. Gone are the days of eating three big meals a day. It was necessary when farmers and most of the population were involved in hard labor, but that is no longer the case for the majority of Westerners.

The new health consciousness is apparent in the number of young people who eat more lightly than their parents. On college campuses eating establishments offer "light fare" options on their menus. For as long as anyone can remember, the golden rule in the West was, "Do what

HINT

A pendulum is a good way to determine what your body needs or even which is the best melon in the produce section of the supermarket. A food item is good for you when the pendulum circles over it in a positive direction. You can practice on the food in your kitchen until you feel confident. Then take your pendulum and head to your favorite store. I actually see more and more people using pendulums to select the freshest or best products with each passing year.

If it is inconvenient to carry a pendulum or you feel too self-conscious using one, there are two methods that do not require any external devices. The first technique uses kinesiology. Have the item you wish to test in your mind. Then make a circle with the thumb and forefinger of your right hand. Hook the forefinger of your left hand in the circle you made with your right hand and pull, to see if you can break the connection. The link will be strong if the food is good for you; if it is not, you will easily break the connection. This is also a good method to use to determine whether you are allergic to certain products.

There is an even more subtle method. Simply extend the forefinger of your dominant hand. Put the end, or pad, of your middle finger on top of the nail on your forefinger. Slide the pad of your middle finger up and down on the nail. It should slide easily if everything is in harmony. If something is not good for you, the nail will become "sticky" or "tacky" and the upper finger will not slide as easily as before.

your parents tell you to do." That included eating what they said to eat, but that is changing with the arrival of so many advanced souls. Humanity must look to them for their wisdom which far exceeds the few years they have been on the planet in this lifetime.

Changes in Exercise Habits

There has been a fitness craze, most noticeably in the United States, for at least thirty years. Large companies have even built exercise facilities for their employees. Studies indicate that less time is taken off from work due to illness when workers participate in exercise programs. Unprecedented numbers of people of all ages are developing a dedication to personal fitness.

Children who are exposed to a wide variety of sports in school develop a habit of enjoying exercise and have the opportunity to discover which sports they prefer. Over time, they can develop the required skills. Confidence in athletic techniques early in life carries over into adulthood. Sports like golf and tennis, once accessible only to the wealthy, have become more widely available. An important discovery children make when exercising or participating in sports is that the concentration required takes their minds off other stresses.

There was a time when the motto of the Western athlete was "no pain, no gain," but this too is changing. The sixties brought an awareness of yoga from the East and greatly influenced how people dealt with their bodies. Instead of painful repetitions and stressed muscles, the body was gently coaxed and lovingly stretched into activity. It was the awakening of the mind-body connection. Many Westerners saw what incredible physical feats could be performed when the mind controlled the breath, heart and muscles.

Changing Religiosity to Spirituality

The typical adult needs help at times in separating religion from spirituality. Christianity has become increasingly fragmented during the past two hundred years[5], and it seems that further divisions become apparent each year. Is there any hope? The new Aquarian recognizes that no single religion holds the only key. That means allowing others the right to their beliefs. It also suggests ending the pressure on missionaries to create converts. Finally, it means acknowledging that all religions have some aspects of merit.

Christianity teaches that unless a person accepts Jesus as his Savior, he cannot go to Heaven. That immediately excludes all Jews, Buddhists, Moslems and millions of others who are not Christian, along with all the wonderful, loving, giving people who never heard of Jesus. In addition, it prohibits all the trillions of humans who lived on Earth before Jesus' arrival from joining the fortunate few. Is this Christian God a god of infinite love? According to this interpretation, that god is a god of love *only to Christians*. Could this be one of the reasons so many Aquarians are staying away from organized religion?

If it were possible to ask all the heads of the major religious orders to set down their *basic* teachings, the truths handed down by the masters and mystics of the past would include only a handful of golden precepts. The two principles common to nearly all religions are love for the Creator or Source or God or whatever name is preferred and love for one another. There is nothing complex or difficult to comprehend. The new spirituality is going back to the foundations of all esoteric teachings. It is rediscovering the simplicity of the ancient instructions given by the masters.

One of the basic tenets of the wisdom teachings was reincarnation. Eastern religions have retained this belief, but it was deliberately deleted from Christian doctrines. Often, Westerners consider the term synonymous with transmigration, which means that the soul, after death, goes into the body of another human or perhaps into an animal. But in reincarnation, the soul incarnates into a human body *which it has created*. This means human souls are themselves; they are the individuated or individualized spirit.

New Agers believe there is evidence in the Bible that reincarnation was originally accepted. Clear references to it were omitted during the Second Council of Constantinople in 553 A.D. because church leaders desired to gain more control over people's lives. The result was that individuals lost their direct connection to God. Jesus asked his disciples who they thought he was (Matt. 16:13-14), and the disciples replied that some said he was Elijah, Jeremiah or one of the prophets, indicating they believed that Jesus was a reincarnation of an early biblical character.

After nearly two thousand years, the Western world is once again considering reincarnation. Only ten years ago people talking about past lives were thought in some circles to be more than a little crazy. Today, many books on the subject are available and prime time television shows are beginning to deal with that theme. Citizens of countries throughout the world are finding it difficult not to believe in the continuity of life. How incredibly unfair it would be for God to give everyone on Earth just one opportunity to learn everything there is to know! How could anyone become perfect in just one lifetime? If it were possible, then the least God could do would be to give each individual an equal chance. That would mean everyone would have to be born under identical circumstances. If God is just, then who decides which soul will enter this physical realm as a crack baby born in the slums of New York City or an AIDS baby born in Bangkok or a Caucasian child born with every advantage to an affluent European couple?

Another reason reincarnation is becoming so widely accepted is that many people are beginning to recall past lives. In addition to remembering, some people are running into "old friends" who trigger shared past-life memories. Not only do certain people seem familiar, but often the circumstances that brought two people together in previous lives are vaguely remembered. New relationships of this sort frequently develop instantaneously, without requiring a period of getting to know one another.

Habits, preferences and dislikes are all present in one's immediate awareness, and there is a feeling of deep harmony and bonding. Often such people are part of one's soul family.

Anyone who has difficulty believing reincarnation is part of the plan on Earth, would do well to talk to a child about having lived before. Children have some amazing stories to tell. Often they have memories of a past-life relationship with a relative who is a personal favorite or with someone for whom they feel a profound dislike in this lifetime. There are also situations in which children react fearfully or negatively to someone they are just meeting "for the first time." Children respond openly and honestly. All these situations indicate a growing awakening among individuals, but is there any noticeable change in the larger picture?

NOTES

1. Riane Eisler. *The Chalice & the Blade.* San Francisco: Harper San Francisco, 1988.

2. Karma refers to the law of opposites or cause and effect that affect this dimension.

3. Patrick Porter, Ph.D. *Awaken the Genius.* Phoenix, AZ: PureLight Publishing Co., 1993. p. 146

4. Joseph Chilton Pearce. *Evolution's End.* San Francisco: Harper San Francisco, 1992

5. Owen C. Thomas. *Attitudes Toward Other Religions.* London: SCM Press, LTD, 1969.

A Global Awakening

Life is really simple, but men insist on making it complicated.

Confucius

The nineties will stand out forever as a decade in which each year has brought increasingly dramatic changes to Earth. One of these days scientists will catch on to what astrologers have been trying to tell them and realize that the planets and constellations far out in the galaxy do affect Earth and every aspect of life.

In 1990 when the planets began lining up in Capricorn, the Berlin Wall came down. The following year the planets went into alignment again and the Soviet Union dissolved. The year after that the diplomats in the Middle East began working on peace negotiations. Those were all events that astonished citizens worldwide; people never thought they would see even one of them occur during their lifetimes, let alone all three within the space of three years. Changes now impact citizens globally.

Issues such as creating shelter for the homeless, providing food for the hungry and overcoming problems arising from pollution should keep citizens of every country — especially the most powerful countries — thinking about their own national problems. Now is the time to resolve issues on the homefront before telling other countries what is best for them or how they should conduct their affairs.

The Global Family

Many of the global activities during the first half of the decade of the nineties have led to a closer connection, a bond among various races and nationalities. Many people are now traveling not only to the countries of their ancestors but also to the places that fascinate them, and such expanded contact creates greater understanding among diverse populations.

Another and even more important factor is becoming quite evident. In the past, people wanted their genetic strains to remain as pure as possible. Young adults were encouraged to marry "one of their own kind," and people tended to prefer their own music, dance, clothing and other artistic expressions. But all that has changed, and the change is due in large measure to people who have lived many lifetimes as members of one race but now are choosing different lineages for this lifetime. For example, many Americans of differing extractions are obsessed with learning Native American traditions such as drumming and living in closer harmony with nature. A desire to relate to Native Americans is also becoming apparent in Europe. Many people are feeling the need to decorate their homes with the art of other cultures. Ethnic foods have become very popular, as have clothing, furniture and, of course, cars from other countries.

Perhaps the greatest interest for the largest number of people is the music of other countries or even of small areas of countries. Many performers now spend a lot of time traveling from one nation to another. It is possible to see entertainers of nearly every nationality performing in many cities, especially cities with universities. A familiar sight in metropolitan areas around the world is the colorful Peruvian street musicians.

(Sometimes I wonder if any are left in Peru.) It is possible to learn much about the people of Madagascar or the aboriginal peoples of Australia through the stories related in their songs. It has been quite popular for young people all over the world to buy CDs of monks chanting hypnotically.

These examples provide ample evidence that the tremendous gap that once existed between cultures is dissolving. Art, theatre, dance, international symposiums and even traveling circuses introduce people of one country to those of another. Fascination with unfamiliar customs, traditions and knowledge bodes well for future recognition and acceptance of one family that encompasses all humanity.

Special Babies

One of the reasons the world is changing so rapidly is that the babies who are now coming into physical existence are very special beings. Most people reading this book are probably aware that divine spirits, or souls, choose to come into this third-dimensional reality, but it might be difficult to understand why anyone would choose to come into the world as a crack baby or an AIDS baby or one born with multiple defects. These babies live only a few hours or months in bodies filled with pain, yet thousands are born every day in every country.

These spirits are performing an important service. They can be divided into two groups. One of these groups is comprised of beings who have chosen to help humanity but have never been in human form. These souls realize it is beneficial for them to experience the emotions of fear, pain, anger, suffering, hunger, and love if they are to offer the greatest possible assistance to humanity. These unselfish souls come into physical bodies, however briefly, to gain greater understanding of human nature.

The entities in the other group come in with such high vibrational frequencies of light that they can raise the vibrations for the entire population. Even if they are here for only a few minutes or a few months, their high energy helps the entire planet. And because these highly evolved souls are arriving in greater numbers in areas where the conditions are the bleakest, they can help bring greater Light to those specific areas. Large city slums all over the globe are now being penetrated with rays of hope, light and love for the first time in many years. These dedicated souls are creating a shift by means of their loving presence.

Decades of Change

There is a Chinese adage that says, "Without change, there is no growth." There seems to be a lot of growth taking place everywhere. More and more people are feeling the need to help those who are struggling, while at the same time they are actively working on themselves. They are feeling a strong need to meditate, to read self-help books and to join groups with similar interests. What prompted this shift?

The way people in the West view the world began to transform about one hundred years ago. There was an awakening to the spirit world, and once again people were seeing Mother Mary and experiencing visitations. Sir Arthur Conan Doyle became well known for trying to contact spirits. Madam Blavatsky and the Theosophists were gaining recognition. Freud, Jung, Adler and Steiner were helping humanity to see themselves differently and to examine their relationships to everything and everyone around them.

Music and art began to express the moment. Innovative modalities and techniques provided new ways to experience creative realities. People stopped wearing "costumes," fashions that had been in vogue for decades. Women gave up their long dresses, tight corsets and impractical hair styles for rapidly changing fashions with flair. Men slowly abandoned their white shirts, black suits, black ties and celluloid collars in favor of more lively hues. Colors splashed from clothing to homes and buildings and into the new world of advertising. People began traveling from continent to continent — not because they were seeking a better life, but as tourists, to see for themselves how other cultures lived. Then television brought the world into everyone's living room. Life kept speeding up. Suddenly, nothing would ever be the same.

But these exciting and positive changes also had their opposite side. The horrors of the First World War shocked citizens when it was learned that entire families living in one town were obliterated by bombs. Then the horrors increased when people discovered the enormity of the Holocaust. One of the results was that the children rebelled by refusing to accept traditional ways. People searched for highs which sometimes led to addiction. Somewhere along the way old-fashioned values like integrity, morality and loyalty lost much of their importance.

Each decade introduced something new to examine. In the twenties Europe and America recovered from World War I. In the thirties the stock market crash and the Great Depression caused many to lose all they had. The Second World War brought a sort of euphoria and a romantic view of what was happening. People in the U.S. were all working in the war effort. Men went off to war gladly to show their patriotism. Most people believed God was on *their* side, whichever side they were on.

In the fifties the atrocities of the world wars and the shock of the atomic bomb were blurring in people's minds. Governments convinced their populations that what had been done had been in their best interests. In general, that belief permeated many lands.

The pervasive optimism that grew during the decade of the fifties flooded into the sixties. Songs and demonstrations all over the globe proclaimed the dawning of the Age of Aquarius. The emotions of the flower children rippled gently, touching all ages and people living in most countries.

A Major Shift

Twenty years later, when the generation of "love children" had near-adult children of their own, the energy again shifted dramatically. Those children (and many of their parents) began calling themselves New Agers. Ask anyone who claims to be a New Ager what he or she was doing in August of 1987 and you will most likely get a very excited answer. People around the world were galvanized by an event known as the Harmonic Convergence. It was a day spent in meditation for a better world that would reflect peace and love. Newspapers and television broadcasts in many countries showed lines of people standing hand in hand for miles, connecting humanity in an unprecedented feeling of oneness, an awareness of working together for a common goal. Others spent the day in small groups, communing or meditating. It was the first time in Earth's long history that so many people had gathered and demonstrated a singleness of purpose. And that purpose was the unification and betterment of all humanity.

It was a time for healing energies to begin flooding the planet. There had been other celebrations in the past but none had reached so many people. Those who took part in the event back in 1987 felt it was a transformational time, not only for themselves personally but also for the whole world. It signaled a period of acceleration and awakening. This united effort toward a better way of life caused the Councils of Light, the governing board of this the Milky Way galaxy, to step up their plans.

Since the eighties life has continued to change even more dramatically. It is now impossible to take anything for granted. As soon as a person puts all his belief into a situation he thinks will last forever, *it is gone!* This is forcing people to change the way they view life.

Formality and social traditions have collapsed into a more natural way of being. The popular way for people to greet one another has moved from not touching at all to shaking hands and now, often, to hugging. Hugs get longer and longer as people share one another's energy. Often New Agers measure whether something was good or bad by the energy they felt. You can hear their comments about experiencing the energy of an event, a place or even a rock.

Language is also reflecting the new attitude. Aquarians have their own vocabulary, which is far more feeling-oriented than left-brained. They like to sign their letters "in Light and love." Often they interject the flavor of Sanskrit or Hindu words and phrases into conversations with each other.

New thoughts have flowed into books. The titles on the bestseller lists over the past few years have been quite amazing and are indicative of a change in thinking. Both the fiction and the nonfiction books that are popular reflect the growing interest in metaphysical subjects. The topics range from angels, UFOs and how to leave the body to manuals on manifesting money. It is difficult not to be a successful author these days if the word "Angel" is included in the title. There are self-help books on every aspect of healing the body, mind and spirit, from breathing and yoga to growing flowers and making essences.

It is quite extraordinary to consider the number of people who are now realizing they have had near-death experiences. Most of these individuals say that in the past the NDE phenomenon was never talked about so they did not realize there was a name for the experience. Certainly, no one could have guessed how many people have crossed over that threshold and returned. By studying them, researchers are gathering evidence of the continuation of life.

Changes in the Medical Community

Humans appear to be no closer to resolving health problems today than they were in the past. Just as one dis-ease seems to be eliminated, another, more virulent one appears. In the twentieth century, the increasing number of inoculations and chemical prescriptions taken by patients is causing the body's natural immunity to disappear. More potent medications must be prescribed as people's systems build up a tolerance or an intolerance to previously administered drugs. Science, with all its advances, has not made great strides in reducing illness or in finding cures. A major concern has always been the regular appearance of plagues, or epidemics, that decimate the population. The challenge of maintaining health and caring for those who are ill is an ongoing problem.

One of today's more serious dilemmas is that people have forgotten how to take responsibility for their own healing. In the past, when people became ill, they went to bed and had time to think about their lives on mental, emotional and spiritual levels. They did some soul searching and in that way could discover the sources of their stress. Now people demand a cure or, short of that, instant relief from pain. Because they pay money, they expect the doctor to make them well again. If patients do not receive what they expect, then they are off to a different doctor who might be more successful. Certain members of the older population in the U.S. often overmedicate by running from one doctor to the next and purposely not mentioning any medications they are already taking. When it comes to drugs, many people believe more is better.

It must be mentioned that much of the blame for this attitude falls on the giant medical associations and pharmaceutical companies around the world. Organizations such as the American Medical Association have done their best for decades to ruin the reputation of any doctor who wants to help patients to heal naturally. Those parents who try to take responsibility for medical crises experienced by their children may be sued by physicians simply because they have refused to accept traditional therapies, regardless of the risk to the child. There was a proposal before the U.S. legislature to track all parents for life if they refuse to inoculate their children. Parents are basing their decision against immunization on the mounting evidence of devastating side effects.

In spite of the many problems, there has been a dramatic change in the medical community in the past couple of years. Doctors who are taking a brave new stance against long-held traditional views of medicine are very much in demand as speakers at conferences around the globe. Some physicians are getting degrees in homeopathy or naturopathy so they can combine traditional allopathic medicine with more holistic methods. These New Age physicians, rather than playing the role of God, are helping patients share responsibility for their wellness. Since the twenties, most doctors have fostered dependence by automatically prescribing medication or surgery in response to illness. Now a few courageous doctors in the U.S. are even buying television time to expose the huge profits gained by pharmaceutical companies from research grants and drug sales. Some doctors are exposing hospitals that advocate unnecessary surgery to boost profit margins as well as exposing attempts by drug companies to suppress alternatives.[1]

Psychologists and sociologists as well as physicians are recognizing the link between mental and emotional problems. Psychotherapists and psychologists in private practice are using innovative techniques, often incorporating meditation, bodywork, energy work, nutrition, movement, Neuro-Linguistic Programming, journaling and art as they interact with their clients. Many body workers such as acupuncturists, Reiki masters and bioenergy therapists dislike hearing their work described as "alternative therapy"; they would prefer the term "compatible therapy." A variety of methods will be used during this transformation period, as one method will work for one person while a different technique will be needed for another.

In the former Soviet Union all doctors have the opportunity to learn psychic healing in addition to traditional medical skills; universities offer two additional years of training in psychic healing. There is one Russian doctor who is presently healing one thousand people at a time. Just as there is a kind of mass hypnosis that renders a portion of a population susceptible to epidemics, there is also a mass susceptibility to healing. The Russian physicians have long realized that a person who is healed in a few minutes will not stay well unless follow-up appointments are kept so he or she can learn the various reasons for having chosen to become ill.

Methods such as Reiki, Mariel and bioenergetics are being taught all over the world. It is common to see people doing Reiki on one another in many countries. Scientists know the body is made of energy. Now research is showing that elevating the vibrations and balancing the electromagnetic field of a body results in dramatic changes. There are wonderful new inventions on the market that alter or normalize these fields. Unfortunately, owners of these devices cannot use them on humans in the Northern Hemisphere for fear of being imprisoned.

In spite of the pressures against seeking natural solutions to physical problems, statistics from the nineties revealed that over fifty per-cent of the U.S. population are now seeking these methods annually. This figure indicates a huge increase over past decades, but it should be noted that the percentages are much higher in the rest of the world. People are becoming discouraged by having to pay so much money to doctors, only to find that their problems persist.

For many years the trend was for doctors to become specialists. Unfortunately, that has resulted in a perception of the body as being made up of separate parts that function independently. Nothing could be further from the truth! But that popular belief has severely hampered the healing process. Patients have had to go to one doctor for one problem and a second doctor for another complication, although everyone is aware of the incredible expense of seeing several specialists. Doctors began to specialize because of the rapidly growing number of physicians in the U.S. A recent statistic revealed that the average doctor has close to seven hundred patients; if one patient were cured every day for two years, the doctor would be out of business. (In China, patients pay for their medical treatment, but if they do not become well quickly or if the problems recur, the physician pays them!)

Many Westerners have become drug-dependent. Media advertising constantly brainwashes the population into believing that all people must get ill and must take medicine to cure their conditions. As a result many individuals are over-medicated.

There is a growing tendency among New Agers to treat abnormal conditions in the body with natural products and alternative treatments whenever possible. People have been amazed by the results! They feel especially rewarded if they have spent years using traditional methods that failed to restore health. In such circumstances it was often the case that they were not only frustrated by the inability to stay healthy but in addition, many had the added trauma of increasingly adverse reactions to pharmaceuticals.

There is certainly a middle ground. Allopathic, or traditional, medicine has its place, but it is of great value to have the services of a forward-thinking physician who will combine holistic methods with traditional medicine. In the future more and more doctors will walk the middle path, while those who cling rigidly to traditional allopathic treatments will have fewer and fewer patients until they are forced to change.

Changes in Media Messages and Performers

For many years it was not considered macho for performers to credit anyone outside themselves for their success. The first time I heard an athlete give credit to God for what he had become, I remember thinking what courage it took. It is one thing to acknowledge his mother as being the driving force behind his success but another to give thanks for the role God has played in his life. Now this kind of recognition is becoming far more commonplace. Many Western people are becoming less shy or less embarrassed about praying publicly.

The message in many television and movie scripts seems to be changing, too, as films concern themselves with themes of life after death or the influence of those beyond the physical realm. Videos designed for children depict death and life between lifetimes. Science fiction stretches the mind's version of reality, expanding the narrow concepts of a third-dimensional world.

Angels have reached a new high in popularity. It is understandable in countries where the population has always accepted the presence of angels, but in the West, that has not been the case. Recent surveys have shown that there are great numbers of people who not only believe in angels but know they have had contact with them.

Changes in Religion and Spirituality

For hundreds of years now the Church, including all its denominations, has become increasingly exclusive. People have chosen a church to match their beliefs, their culture, their race and even their social status in the community. Some people felt it was necessary to have a visible affiliation with a church in order to maintain the appearance of "doing God's work."

Much of the hypocrisy found in the Church is now under scrutiny. As a result, organized religion is experiencing a great fracture right down the middle. The fundamentalists are becoming even more inflexible. In an effort to keep parishioners from straying further, stricter rules are being established. New Agers and any other people espousing freedom from structure, narrow-minded thinking and subservience are condemned by the Church as representing Satan.

This attempt to control the membership began thousands of years ago when people were first taught they were not worthy to speak to God directly. Men established themselves as priests who would be the intercessors between humans and God — for payment, of course. Great suffering has resulted from this separation, as people felt unworthy to include God as a part of them. God, their Father, the old man with the long white beard, was always up there somewhere, critically judging pitiful humans down here. Nobody could achieve the level of perfection that was required of them. Because only men could become priests, women were relegated to secondary roles. Slowly the Church took away the rights of females until they became little more than property. Women suffered as second-class citizens for a very long time.

In many denominations changes are now occurring that allow women to take their vows. This movement is also reflected in the present rethinking of the role played by Mary, the mother of Jesus. A new understanding has evolved regarding the phrase "Immaculate Concept" as opposed to "Immaculate Conception." Many people now believe Mary's purpose was to offer Jesus the greatest possible assistance so he could fulfill his destiny by becoming the model for ascension. To do this, Mary had to carry the "immaculate concept" of her son in her heart. She could not afford moments of doubt or despair, regardless of the circumstances. It was her role to hold high the image of her son's perfection. Jesus needs her help on the physical plane to keep his purpose for coming here foremost in his life. This perspective, along with soon-to-be-revealed information regarding Jesus' female disciples, will balance the importance of males and females in Christian traditions.

Humanity is discovering that in the same way that Jesus was the Son of God, so all people are sons and daughters of God. What the fundamentalists do not want people to believe is that God is within everyone and that all humans are sparks of the divine. But the truth of that statement is presented very clearly in the New Testament. Jesus said, "God is in His Holy Temple," and when asked where that temple was located, he replied, "The temple of God is within." Many leaders of religious institutions are afraid that if the public realizes this, there will be no further place for them or their churches.

It is important to realize that the two-thousand-year-old statement about being sons and daughters of God was expressed at the level of understanding appropriate for that time. Modern rationale suggests that no one truly is a son or daughter of a Father God or even of a Father/Mother God. Everyone is God! That is the next step in evolutionary thinking. Jesus tried to teach many concepts that are only now being understood.

Jesus, Buddha, Kukulkan, Saint Germain, Krishna and many others came into physical bodies at various times to set examples for humanity. Most of what they taught was understood by very few until recently. The visionary teachings of ancient wisdom were distorted as they went through translation from one language to another. In some instances, the writings were purposely biased as one religious leader or another wanted his personal beliefs to be reflected in the religious teachings of the time.

Much of the most profound information was withheld from the people. Leaders of the hierarchical religions believed it would be in the best interests of the congregations if they were kept in ignorance. For example, *The Gospel of Thomas*[1] was only one of the many books omitted from the New Testament, because in it Jesus is not performing miracles or fulfilling prophecy; rather, he is offering wisdom through his insights. This book does not contain the narrative style of the other gospels but is a collection of one hundred fourteen sayings of Jesus.

A recent example of the withholding of information from the masses can be seen in the Dead Sea Scrolls. They were discovered in Upper Egypt in 1945, but only recently did the bulk of the contents become available to the general public. A recent television documentary revealed that total accessibility of the scrolls came about only because one individual broke the computer code. Until that time only a limited number of religious scholars had seen most of the historical documents. Such secrecy will end when additional ancient scrolls are discovered.

Many church leaders are realizing, too, that services must be changed so their focus is on *serving* the needs of the congregation. Messages must uplift rather than dwell on sin, Satan and punishment for not following man-made rules. A religion of service, regardless of denomination, is one of singing, dancing, laughter, deep involvement, great understanding and no prejudice among its members. Parishes are teaching techniques such as meditation, stress reduction, the development of prosperity consciousness and alternative modalities of healing. For the first time in many centuries people are attending services because they feel better for having done so, rather than because they are afraid of going to Hell if they do not attend.

This new freedom is clearly evidenced by the comfortable clothes people are now wearing to church. Worshipers are realizing that God is not judging them, especially for the outfits they are wearing. It is also apparent in the increased attendance at progressive churches.

Another interesting phenomenon regarding organized religion in the West, is that there are now two generations of children who have grown up, in many cases, with no religious background at all. They do not realize that the churches' God is up there disapproving of them if they do something "wrong" in the eyes of the church or even that they are supposed to be living in "the end times." They are certainly not as innocent or gullible as their grandparents were and they are far more sophisticated. Perhaps that is because the present generation receives as much information in one day as their grandparents received in a lifetime. Young people are often more discerning and more accepting than previous generations; sometimes elders discover they are learning from the younger generation, rather than teaching them.

For thirty years the West has been absorbing various practices from Eastern religions, and they are being blended with Western styles of worship. Humanity is bound to benefit from this combination. Both East and West teachings are to love God and to love one another; it is only the man-made laws that are so diverse and often in conflict with each other. Life would be dramatically changed if all people lived life according to these two simple rules.

A Redefining of Roles

People are finally beginning to realize that all humans are miniature universes, and that is fostering a new sense of belonging. God is in the planets and stars; the Creative Force, the Divine Spirit, exists within everyone and everything. No one ever needs to feel alone again. Many groups gather weekly to pray for peace or to meditate on the healing of the planet, and that action automatically connects them with all other groups or individuals who have similar goals.

Lightworkers are a fast-growing group of world servers. They have awakened to the realization that they chose to be in physical form at this momentous time of transformation. A common characteristic among Lightworkers is the need to be of service. Many are quickly becoming teachers, healers and advisors who work not only in their immediate vicinities but all over the world. Most will tell you they have changed professions but that all their past experiences led them to where they are right now. These special individuals are willing to help whenever and wherever they can.

A large majority of Lightworkers do not yet know their purpose or their specific area of work for the changing times. This is often true because what they will be doing has not yet been discovered or invented or it is too soon for a particular talent to blossom. For example, a friend, whom no one knew could sing, recently sang for a group. When he had finished, everyone felt much more balanced, energized and free of stress than they had before he sang. It might well be that he was meant to heal with his voice. Most Lightworkers who are already on their paths say that when the time is right, the proper door opens. In addition, people will not be working toward just one goal in the coming years; humans are multitalented, and in the future the goal will be to develop every potential so that the species can become all it is capable of becoming.

Problems and Solutions

Life has not progressed in accordance with the optimistic predictions of the forties. It was believed then that by the end of the century people in developed countries would be working only three days per week and that their biggest problem would be what to do with all their leisure time. But in spite of modern conveniences, the average person has less personal time than ever for relaxation.

One of the problems is the Industrial Age — the faster machines produce, the faster humans work to keep up with the output. Another problem is that companies are downsizing their staffs, which often results in the dismissal of senior executives. The executives have very little opportunity for future employment because so many other businesses are doing the same thing and because they are overqualified for nearly all positions. Such a policy requires remaining employees to work additional hours to compensate for staff reductions.

Gone are the days when women automatically stayed home to raise the children. Their lives have become far more complex as they try to balance traditional roles with new demands. Westerners seem to have a pervasive need to be doing something nearly every minute, combined with a compulsive drive to amass additional material goods and the need to become more than they already are. This obsessive behavior has carried over to the rearing of children. Seldom are they allowed to just play or simply to be. Instead, parents push them into structured recreation where there is an underlying message that says they should be continuously pursuing a goal.

In spite of ongoing research, no one has come up with a simple, acceptable method of reducing the number of unplanned pregnancies. With the birth rate climbing steadily higher, Earth is quickly becoming overpopulated, which is leading to shortages of food and housing. It is certain that life has not become simpler as a result of the latest inventions. In fact, many scientific achievements are worsening conditions by contributing to the pollution level. The twentieth century was supposed to be a period when the problems of Earth would be greatly reduced. Instead, humanity finds itself confronted by more serious problems than ever before.

In the past citizens looked to their governments to resolve their nations' problems. Now people are questioning the information being given them by their government representatives. No longer are they trustingly accepting as truth everything they are told. Increasing evidence suggests the existence of numerous governmental cover-ups. In the months and years to come, citizens will discover just how much information has been withheld because government officials have believed that the average person could not handle the truth. This attitude on the part of many officials holds people back from personal growth and acceptance of change. When the protective arm becomes too strong, the response is no longer submissiveness but rebellion.

If science and government cannot resolve humanity's worst dilemmas, it might be advantageous to look at problems from a different perspective. When solutions cannot be found in the outside world, the clear message is to look within. It is time to take personal responsibility. Conditioned reactions have been a part of the human response to daily stress for such a long time that it will be necessary to change the collective consciousness. That can be done only little by little and on a day-to-day basis. Many New Agers are already experiencing the need to become conscious of their thoughts as well as of their actions. Growing numbers of people are searching for alternative methods for dealing with every aspect of daily living.

For example, people are beginning to live in houses that do not tax the environment. In the South especially, communities of like-minded individuals are building straw-bale houses. These energy-efficient homes stay warm in the winter and cool in the summer. People in these communities look out for one another and are always there when help is needed, forming associations made up of couples, families and singles. The need to be with consonant people is certainly increasing. Attempts at communal living in the nineties will establish the prototypes for the communities of Light that will spring up around the world in the near future.

Many people are experiencing extreme frustration because there is no road map to show them where they are headed. Earth is not giving them a plan to follow, and the only thing they can count on is the awareness that everything is changing. But the help everyone needs is coming.

---

1. James P. Carter, M.D., Dr. P.H. *Racketeering In Medicine: The Suppression of Alternatives.* Norfolk: Hampton Roads Publishing Company, Inc., 1993.

The Sighting

We are all parts of an infinite plan which is wholly wise and good.
Richard Maurice Bucke

The day begins just like any other. Parents are awakening and helping children get ready for school. Those who have jobs away from their homes are busily making necessary preparations. The work day starts and everyone is following the usual routine. Then slowly, a unique feeling begins to invade each person's consciousness. The more a person tries to dismiss it from his awareness, the more persistent it becomes.

Finally, a moment arises when the urgings become too powerful to ignore. As strange as it seems, everyone feels the need to go outdoors. People walk outside of their homes. Those who work in metropolitan areas take elevators down to the ground floors of skyscrapers. The desire to speak is strangely absent. Groups of people move in silence. Everyone seems to be in his own space, oblivious to the people and things around him. Many individuals are not even consciously aware that they have walked outside; they simply arrive at the awareness that they are standing in front of the buildings they had been in.

Even those who are driving along busy streets and highways have the compelling need to stop their vehicles and get out. Drivers look for places to pull over and park along freeways. They wonder vaguely why they are acting in such a strange manner but that thought does not stop them from continuing with their actions. Others who are standing outside houses and buildings briefly question what they are doing and why. Some people have the experience they are watching themselves, but they have no desire to stop whatever is happening. People feel an increasing need to be at a certain destination and that supersedes all other thoughts.

The next overwhelming urge is to look up into the sky. High in the heavens small circles of light begin to appear. The rational mind tries to identify these unusual objects, and people who have seen parachute landings think initially that the hundreds of small circles are parachutes coming down to Earth. But as they continue to watch, the circles begin to transform, appearing to be soap bubbles of iridescent Light. These orbs grow larger as they approach the ground. Sunlight shimmers on them and rainbow-colored rays radiate from the spheres. Some of the spheres take on the form of more complex geometries of Light. People everywhere watch in silent fascination. There is a stillness, a calm, a sense of intense yet peaceful beauty that pervades the entire scene of the watchers and the watched. Slowly, the orbs and other geometric Light formations drift downward and gently touch the Earth. Although they seem to be swept gently along on currents of wind, the iridescent bubbles all seem to have very specific destinations.

Next, an even more astonishing development occurs and it repeats over and over again. One by one, each Light formation touches the ground. Slowly, a human form becomes visible. Then another and another can be seen through the soft yet intense Light. Perception seems to shift from seeing only beautiful Lights to seeing beautiful *beings of Light*. Methodically people's minds begin to grasp the reality that they are seeing human-type *beings* who are more beautiful than could have been imagined previously and who exemplify an exquisite level of perfection.

Still no one feels like speaking. The experience is simply too breathtaking. It seems as though time has shifted. Has the event been occurring over the span of two minutes or two hours? It is impossible to know. The scene is too awe-inspiring to be rationalized by the logical brain. Later, it will be remembered by some of the people watching that they had heard heavenly choirs singing celestial music, music that sounded as though all the angels in the universe had gathered and were rejoicing in song. The entire incident will seem to have been a light and sound show of unsurpassed excellence.

Every Lightworker, world-server, starseed and ordinary individual striving to be a better person is now being greeted by these Lightbeings. In truth, every human is being met by those who have always guided them from the other side of the vibrational veil, yet there are those in every city of every nation who cannot see the arrival of these precious individuals. The people who are choosing not to see, wish to keep life the same as it has always been. The past is comfortable for them and they consider change to be painful or frightening, so try though they might, the logical mind will not permit them to see what is actually here. They are choosing to close down their vision of this new reality.

But billions are able to see these advanced beings. Many young children recognize Lightbeings before adults do, for they have not yet closed down their ability to see beyond third-dimensional limitations. Babies and toddlers smile or laugh with joy. Teens express mixed emotions which range from "It's about time!" to "I can't believe this is really happening." Many adults are even more conflicted. Their rational minds cannot explain away these extraordinary events. At first many individuals appear confused and bewildered. Others begin to laugh, cry tears of joy, jump up and down or dance to express their delirious rapture.

This unfolding scene brings bliss beyond any previous experience on Earth. The many years of loneliness and separation vanish in a few seconds as the Lightbeings approach. For some people there is instant recognition of a guide, teacher or spiritual healer from the other side. Others respond, "So that's what you look like!" Many are met by more than one guide. At some deep level most people acknowledge that help has arrived.

When such a magnificent being looks at a person with eyes beaming pure love and a heart radiating goodness and acceptance, wave after wave of chills flow through the body, confirming the presence of the highest teachers, guides and ascended masters. The reverberating waves also serve to raise a person's vibrational frequency. The Beings of Light had to step-down their frequencies as they descended into denser matter so they might accommodate the slower vibrational field of Earth. Each human experiences an elevation in the frequency of his subtle bodies as his energies synchronize with those of the Lightbeings.

Their bodies remain translucent and they appear to radiate a luminescence. The edges of their physical bodies seem less discernible than are humans' and they appear to glow with rainbow colors. These special beings call to mind the appearance of Jesus, the Christ, after his resurrection, or transformation. The disciples had difficulty recognizing him because he was radiant and more etheric.

This amazing occurrence is being repeated all over the world as the advanced beings use their abilities to appear everywhere simultaneously and, often, holographically. No one can convince those choosing not to see that this event is actually taking place; the experience is available, however, to all those who desire to go forward with Earth into the fifth dimension. Those individuals are able to see the descension of the many masters who have always watched over Earth and cared dearly for her inhabitants.

Suddenly the emotions overflow. Many people experience tears of joy along with laughter. Most of humanity, for the first time they can remember, feel a complete sense of belonging. The overwhelming sensation of love for everyone and everything pulls all awareness into the *now*. There is an absence of judgment against those who seem unable to share the experience. No one is commenting, "I can see what is happening, why can't you?" The impression is a recognition that all people are one, in spite of their individuality.

The feeling of being family fills people with even more Light. As they look out into the distance, they watch in amazement as their lights connect with thousands of other Lights. Together, humanity appears to be creating a grid of Light on the surface of the planet. As more links occur, the Lights flash and glisten ever brighter. Some people send out rays of a particular hue that stretch out and connect with similar rays. As cobalt blue joins cobalt blue, and magenta unites with magenta, a sensation arises in the heart center that makes a person aware that he is connecting with a member of his soul family.

As the Light grids radiate out to distant stars and planets, sensations of warmth and belonging flood a person's body, and he realizes that he has just reconnected to those distant realms which are also his home. Next, he becomes aware that Light and love are flowing out through his feet down to the heart of Mother Earth as he expresses his gratitude in a fifth-dimensional way. Sending Light and love is a superior method of expressing feelings, for without words there can be no misunderstandings.

No one wants this sensation to end, for it is so unusual to feel immersed in loving compassion for all things. The radiance of the moment slowly creeps into the collective consciousness. Gently an awareness of this reality causes a person to shift his focus. Everything is shining — the trees, hills, water, rocks and grass. Even man-made objects like cars and buildings seem to glisten, although not as much as nature. A tranquil realization floods the consciousness; there is a knowing that nothing on this plane of reality will revert to the way it was. Everything in the world has been shifted a little farther into the next dimension.

Another deep wave of emotion flows from each person's heart down into the crystal at the center of the Earth. As soon as one human senses this feeling pouring out from his heart, he knows that millions of other humans are having the same experience. The heart muscle begins beating in synchrony with the heartbeat of the Earth Mother. A tremendous up-welling of love from the ground, from Gaia, enters the body through the soles of the feet, and oneness with Earth is achieved.

That sensation then slowly gives way to an awareness of a screen on which holographic images are appearing to each person. The imaging begins with scenes of Earth's creation. Deep feelings are aroused as each viewer vibrates with a beautiful soul form that appears holographically. Immediately each person recognizes the radiance to be himself or herself in soul form!

It is time to further understand the part each one played in Earth's history. A long time ago a group of souls decided to experiment with density on a tiny planet called Earth. Each soul's first creation was a mental body. After the two learned to interact and function successfully together, all the mental bodies agreed to cooperate with the Lords of Creation. As had been the custom on similar planets, the lords requested the help of the mental bodies in establishing a mineral kingdom on Earth, and the mental selves agreed. It was to be the next great step in the evolution of the planet.

Detailed holographic images show the process of selecting combinations of elements that will grow, evolve and transform deep within the Earth. Minerals are cultivated and tended by the spirits and devas of the mineral kingdom. The images reveal an underground laboratory of experimentation in which millions of combinations of colors and textures exist. Specimens of minerals grow like flowers deep within Earth and many of them have never been seen by anyone in a physical body. Gems and minerals continuously heave up to the surface as human energy levels evolve enough to tolerate their higher vibrations.

Now, holographic images are revealing the effects of toxic waste from nuclear dumps deep in the Earth, along with the damage done by atomic bombs and underground nuclear testing. There is a creaking and groaning of the tectonic plates as they grate against one another rather than easily sliding while following the rhythmic undulations of the planet. Prior to the twentieth century, abundant oil deposits lubricated the plates but with each passing year there is less oil, so plate slippage now jars every land mass, creating deep rends on Earth's surface. The next images testify to the greed of most humans who mine gemstones and minerals. They destroy and thereby sacrifice large mineral fields with their dynamite blasts in order to extract a few prize specimens. On this planet mining has seldom been done lovingly.

The holograms then demonstrate how crystals will be used in the years to come. They are great amplifiers of energy, and in the future crystals will be used in healing centers to amplify light and sound, just as they were in the past. It is possible for them to grow very quickly and also to multiply. They can be programmed to radiate colors the human eye cannot yet see. Crystals can send, receive and store information. Giant recordkeeper crystals are just beginning to surface.

All minerals are in the process of evolution but their growth has been severely hampered by destruction on every continent over the past half-century. Even the crudest stone is progressing toward becoming a diamond. What pleases the mineral kingdom most is the discovery of the unique properties of crystals by New Agers. It is really the first time in the collective consciousness of the mineral kingdom that they have felt loved!

Then a wave of awareness forms a mind link between each person and the plant kingdom. The holographic images reveal the time period when the souls were creating emotional or astral bodies. Later those bodies began working with the Lords of Creation to establish the plant kingdom. Here, too, there is an almost infinite variety of color and texture and adaptability. Many swiftly projected holographic images show the plant kingdom progressing from the first algae that appeared in primordial waters and evolving into lush green tropical vegetation. Since that time plants and trees of all varieties have continued to develop, manifesting greater complexity and breathtaking colors.

As each person watches the pictures fast-forwarding to the present, he becomes aware of a subtle movement that seems to hover in, under and around the plant kingdom. As the images show this motion in greater focus, he is amazed and fascinated to witness the beauty of the devic kingdom which oversees all plant life. The devas, gnomes, brownies and sprites literally wring their hands as the giant trees cry in pain. The observer connects his heart to the spirits of the giant redwood trees, to special areas like the Black Forest in Germany and the jungles of Brazil. He, too, feels pain as the plant kingdom struggles to get sufficient sunlight, while pollution nearly suffocates the pores of their leaves.

This scenario is followed by an even more intense pain as each person watches the deforestation of the planet. It is apparent that the spirits of the larger trees cooperate with the devas who are still trying to maintain the delicate balance within all of nature. And again, it is apparent that there is no judgment coming from the devas, only love and deep concern. What a lesson this is for humanity!

A new sensation now penetrates the consciousness of each individual as the images fade and change. They watch the scenes as the souls decide to continue their experiment in density. The mental bodies were doing very well working with the mineral kingdom, and the astral/emotional bodies were extremely busy with the evolving plant kingdom, but further density was necessary to fully inhabit and utilize a third-dimensional reality. That could be achieved only through the creation of an etheric body upon which the physical body could pattern itself, so that step was accomplished next.

Not long afterward, the Lords of Creation determined that it was time to establish an animal kingdom suitable for Earth. That would indeed be a tremendous challenge for the physical selves. Slowly images appear in holographic form showing the deliberate creation and experimentation within the evolving animal kingdom.

For the first time each person is seeing animals differently: they appear to be like little children trying to please humans. Animals that are in close contact with people do their best to emulate them. Most of them have no thought of self, and they try to take away human illness, suffering and pain by absorbing the negativity into their auras. Domesticated animals and pets so closely associate with their human families that they eventually contract the same diseases; that is how deeply they aspire to become human. Recollections arise in the mind of each person of times when he or she has been less than kind or patient with them.

Humanity has enslaved many animals and kept them in captivity. Their evolutionary progress has virtually been stopped, for humans have never considered the possibility that animals could become more than what they were at the moment. Each person senses the sacrificial attitude of the more highly evolved mammals, realizing that they will take on whatever role is necessary for them to help the planet.

It becomes very clear that many dolphins and whales have brains that are superior to humans, brains and bodies that are more highly evolved. However, they have chosen lives of service and sacrifice, absorbing human negativity to help ease the overwhelming burdens on Mother Earth. Oh, the heart pain that is felt for the animals as thousands of years of human subjugation and mishandling seem to pass through the cellular memory of each person. But as quickly as those thoughts come in, they flow out again. The collective consciousness begins clearing its RNA/DNA patterning. After many ages the new humanity is becoming filled with a sense of loving obligation, realizing they must be custodial guardians caring for and nurturing the animal kingdom.

Suddenly it is so apparent! Every single subatomic particle on and in this planet is necessary to her balance. Every system was slowly and deliberately created to work in harmony with everything else. Each person's mind wonders how humans could have deceived themselves into believing that the continuous rape of Earth would have no repercussions. Could it be that humans have thought of themselves as being separate from Source for so long that they have also believed that everything else is separate? Nothing could be further from the truth. It has been said that the flutter of a butterfly's wings in the Pacific can cause a hurricane in the Atlantic. It is critical to Earth's survival that every human become aware that all aspects of Earth have consciousness — from the oceans and the trees to the energy vibrations of which they are made.

It is no longer acceptable to participate in a world bent on amassing material goods at the expense of all the other kingdoms, which are as much a part of Earth as humans are. Each person's awakening vision sees that every accomplishment that is a symbol of humanity's progress destroys Earth in some way. All methods of transportation deplete Earth's supply of fossil fuels. The need for wood to make homes, buildings and furniture, along with paper products, destroys acres of forest. The increasing need for energy — from electricity, gas and nuclear power — creates pollution both above and below the surface of Earth. How could humans be so blind? Why would humanity allow such a system to develop when it creates an escalating misappropriation of natural resources? The greedy cartels and conglomerates continue to seize even greater control.

Then the focus shifts to those who really care, the ones who truly love the land. They can be found in every nation. These people feel deep concern for the growing problems and wish to help in any way they can. There is the thought of banding together to protest and to fight the injustices of the world. But immediately there is a strong reaction from all the kingdoms: that reaction is love! Collectively, they send the message that it is no longer appropriate to protest or to fight for what is considered right. That has been tried for thousands of years and the only result has been more fighting.

Now is the time to think with and act from the heart. No judgment. No violence. The only responsible reaction is to surround negative actions with love. Once a person gains this perspective, he operates from a place of inner peace in which every outward action is the result of the inward knowingness of pure love. Others want to know his secret, wondering what he is doing that is making him so happy, and they want to be in his presence so that the tranquility and joy will radiate to their beings.

This experience has enlarged each person's vision. For a moment the vistas of life as they really exist were opened, and it was one of the few occasions when mind and ego did not distort reality. At that time the basic patterning in the RNA/DNA was transformed from separatism to unity.

Humanity has moved beyond relying on ego for survival. It was ego that long ago created the sense of duality. The first stage of human evolvement was, according to the ancient teachings, "Man, know thyself,"[1] and that could be accomplished only through separation and egoism. Now it is important to recognize with all senses that the majority of people have completed their first great step.

The next stage of human evolution is the integration of the soul. It is in this initiation that humans must learn the other ancient teaching: "Man, forget thyself." It is the dawn of the age of brotherhood when humans exist in loving relationship with the living and the nonliving, the great and the minute. People sense that each of them is one unit of the great collective. Every deed and action begins to be carried out from the perspective of how others will be affected. Most humans are realizing during this period that God is within as well as without. They are discovering their God-like abilities. This is the knowledge that will bring about the thousand years of peace. Following very swiftly upon that stage is the third stage, during which the spirit of humanity becomes fully integrated. Then the fusion of all of consciousness will be complete. People will have stopped asking God for favors in their prayers and they will have stopped trying to be God-like, for they will truly know they are God. It will have become impossible to see anything as being outside of God. From this new perspective, everything that happens is either love or a lesson in love.

But in the meantime each person must ask whether there is something he should be doing with his life. How is a person to know what that something is? It is comforting to realize that everyone has already moved deeply into the process of Ascension. The next chapters will help to provide an indication of how far humanity has already come and to guide the reader to living life more fully and blissfully in the days ahead.

---

1. Alice A. Bailey. A *Treatise on the Seven Rays*. New York: Lucis Publishing Company, 1982.

New Perspectives

You live in illusion and the appearance of things.
There is a reality, but you do not know this.
When you understand this, you will see that you are nothing,
and being nothing, you are everything.

Kalu Rinpoche

Earth's population is witnessing a greater period of change in a shorter period of time than even the Spiritual Hierarchy of the planet had envisioned. There are predictions that between now and the year 2000 the world will experience at least ten thousand years' worth of evolutionary progress. What will that mean?

The greatest change will be in consciousness. For thousands of years humanity has lived in a minute portion of reality. Individuals have created their little corners of the world to be just the way they thought they should be. The farmers' world has been one reality. The people who work and play in New York City, London and Tokyo all have had their realities, while rock stars and world-renowned athletes have lived in another reality altogether. The way people view life has always depended upon how they interpret their daily experiences.

In this age of information it is now possible not only to see other people's realities but also to begin to understand them. For years it has been the norm for an individual to center his or her interest upon career, family and possibly a hobby. Now those who have access to computers are able to cruise the Internet and learn all the current information on any subject, and that information is available to inhabitants in every country on Earth. People are expanding their horizons and broadening their perspectives.

C. Jung's term, "collective unconscious," refers to energy that is made up of the attitudes, beliefs, interpretations and feelings of the world's population. This collective energy defines what is real and what is not real for the people existing in a particular time and place. In the past, race, nationality, gender, social status, religion and education have been some of the aspects that have developed localized characteristics of consciousness. When these various facets of reality are added together, they form the collective unconscious.

At this time the collective is not only rapidly changing but is also rapidly expanding. The drug experimentation of the sixties immediately altered reality for the entire planet. There has been continuous experimentation with drugs over the past fifty years, especially under the auspices of governmental research. In addition to artificially induced altered states of consciousness, many "normal" people have become interested in meditation, pranic breathing[1] or, more recently, Holotropic Breathwork,[2] jogging and yoga, not to forget hypnosis and the many forms of release therapy. All these and many more take the practitioner into other realities and other realms of consciousness.

Many parallel realities exist on Earth now. Most are not separate or distinct but, like the ages and the dimensions, they overlap and interpenetrate one another. The relationship among these realities is constantly in the process of change as humanity's views on a particular topic fluctuate.

Extraterrestrials

The subject of extraterrestrials provides a good example of parallel realities. There are still people who believe no life exists beyond Earth, and that is their reality. Others have read books and seen television reports about alien life forms and believe they could exist. Still another group of people have seen spacecraft for themselves and have perhaps even been aboard a ship.

The public has been told that the majority of people in the last category have had experiences that have not been overwhelmingly pleasant. Why? What has been the collective thought regarding beings from beyond Earth? Especially if they did not have a human appearance? Fear. Consensus reality says that all extraterrestrials are sinister and out to subjugate humanity in order to take over the planet.

Abductions by Aliens

It will be understood shortly that a group of humans have agreed to continue life on the third-dimensional level with the help of alien beings from several different planetary systems. Overwhelmingly negative information has been spread about this project, but the experiment was designed to improve existing races through the hybridization of the species.

For example, the Grays are reported to have become unable to experience emotions due to the atrophying of their emotional bodies through disuse and also to have lost the ability to reproduce. In contrast, many humans are very emotional and are reproducing irresponsibly. This mutually agreed-upon project is intended to create a race with the advanced abilities of the Grays and the positive attributes of humans. Those who have agreed to take part in the experiment realized they were not yet ready to move into the fifth dimension on Earth's timetable, so they agreed to this grand experiment in another third-dimensional situation. For many years these special people have been learning to adjust to life on spaceships in preparation for their journey to their new home planet. In truth, the abductees are pioneers who have agreed to settle a New Earth, having made that decision at higher levels of being. Aliens involved in the project believe they are helping humanity as well as themselves; it is not a purely selfish venture as people are often led to believe. Of course, it must be admitted that there are some extraterrestrials who might have believed they were operating with the best of intentions but who have acted ruthless or unfeeling when judged by human standards. They are not the extraterrestrials under discussion here. Some of the aliens are genetically creating human/alien offspring for the purpose of producing a race of mentally, physically and emotionally superior beings. Many of these extraterrestrials can still reproduce their own kind, and they have a high moral code. Their ethics will not allow them to have sexual relations with a human if it is contrary to an individual's freely made decision.

It must be pointed out that nearly all women would have negative responses to alien sexual encounters because of moral and religious teachings. For example, if a woman told her partner she had been up on the ship again last night and had had great sex, she would be institutionalized! At the present time it is in the best interest of both sexes to believe that such a bizarre experience could scarcely be viewed as one of great bliss.

Testimonies of both men and women report a cold, clinical approach to experimentation and conception on the ships. It must be remembered that fear creates and increases pain. In addition, the fear-based reactions are understandable because more than ninety-nine percent of human conditioning has been that they are the "good guys" and that every extraterrestrial is interested only in controlling humanity.

Undoubtedly, not every visitor from another planet is more highly evolved morally and mentally than humans. Therefore, it is likely that some people have encountered aliens who may not have progressed beyond the lowest stratum[3] of the third dimension. However, at the present time it is virtually impossible for these lower third-dimensional beings to tolerate Earth's heightened vibrational field as the planet begins to overlap the third and fifth planes.

It is interesting that world-servers and Lightworkers never seem to report having the kind of negative experience that would be labeled an abduction, although many talk about their wonderful experiences up on the ships. I would suggest that this is because they are not a part of any experiment to continue life in a third-dimensional reality. Most Lightworkers believe they have come here at this time to move forward with Earth as she births into a higher dimension.

It is important to realize that the intention of the project is to produce babies who will be superior to *both* parents. Experimentation such as this has always existed, on Earth and elsewhere. All humans who have agreed to participate in the initial settling of the New Earth know their own ships and have been aboard many times. It will be learned that most often this enormous decision was made before birth and these people have been traveling to the ships since they were very young. Both men and women are becoming increasingly aware of holding their babies while visiting the ships. Humans are establishing relationships and families with their new partners. Periodically, they are questioned to see if it is still their intention to immigrate to the New Earth.

Many of the extraterrestrials involved in this project are extremely concerned about human well-being. One of the considerate and compassionate plans they have for their human families is to provide surroundings that are as familiar as possible. To create another Earth, it is necessary to gather plant and animal specimens for future adaptation. Those who are botanical experts are gathering samples for transplanting on their distant "New Earth." Others are experimenting with some of the animals here so they might adapt to a new and different environment.

Cattle Mutilations

The results of their animal experimentation have been labeled "cattle mutilations." It is not the intent of extraterrestrials to kill animals for pleasure, sport or food (as do humans) but rather to collect genetic information so that selected animals might be able to adapt to their new world. The goal is simply to help the animals adjust to life on the ships and in their future locations.

Alien beings from other star systems observe humans slaughtering animals by the millions daily. The human species undervalues life in all sectors, from cutting down forests to overgrazing land and polluting rivers and oceans with industrial waste. They observe hunters and fishermen who kill for the sport of it. Visitors from other planets watch as many people gluttonously consume huge and unnecessary amounts of food and notice that leftovers are thrown into garbage cans, while in other areas millions of people are too weak from starvation even to cry. They are aware of the incredible waste by consumer-oriented societies. It is difficult for them to understand humans who react dramatically to a few animals being used for genetic research.

It is curious that many people who react vehemently to animal experimentation eat animals daily, wear leather clothing and use other animal products. Many humans have judged their space neighbors to be barbaric, but extraterrestrials have every right to think that the majority of humans are primitive and unfeeling. They are convinced humans have a strange sense of morality.

It is very important to understand that the animal species that are being tested for future relocation have already agreed to the plan through their group consciousness. Humans must learn and accept the fact that many species of animals are now leaving the planet. Some animal groups are not sufficiently evolved to move forward, so they will continue life in another third-dimensional place. Plant and animal groups have already made their decisions, so every year more are becoming extinct. All human efforts to "save" them will be in vain, as they cannot and will not survive the coming changes.

A Best-Case Scenario

During the coming years, the true meaning of duality and illusion will become increasingly apparent as humanity begins to experience two very opposite realities. For one segment of the population, there will be increasing chaos in which nothing seems to work and life is a constant struggle to survive. It will be impossible for those experiencing utter confusion and disorder to see beyond the world of illusion — which they are creating. They will believe everyone is out to get them. It will seem very apparent to them that they are about to lose their jobs, their homes, their money and their partners. Each day will seem to bring greater fear. They will have difficulty sleeping, and the food they eat will not be properly digested. A combination of headaches, chest pains, backaches and digestive problems including ulcers will manifest periodically. As they believe the boss, the car salesperson and the government are out to get them, so it will be. Their fears will create their realities.

Existing temporarily in this scene will be another picture of reality altogether. A second group of humanity is discovering greater joy, deeper peace and an inexplicable optimism about the future. Each day brings a growing sense of destiny. These people know their time is coming. They realize these are the times and events they came to witness. Personal and global disasters seem to pass right by these individuals. They feel as though they are living in a protective bubble. This group is not preoccupied with individual survival. Rather, their great need is to be of service. They are willing to work for the benefit of all and are directing energy toward the healing of the planet. More than any other attribute, they are learning to be flexible and to face whatever circumstance develops. It is easy to understand that the distance between the two groups is growing greater with each passing day.

UFOs

The future is always uncertain but the next three to five years will determine what course the Earth changes will take. For some time now there have been ships (UFOs) waiting to escort to safety all Lightworkers and indeed all those with a sufficiently high vibration, should it become necessary to evacuate Earth for a short period of time. Many highly visible ships are constantly in the skies over Mexico, especially around Mexico City. It is believed they are there because of a possible volcanic eruption, in which case these UFOs would be in a position to lift up many members of the enormous population.

Small ships are used to shuttle people to huge mother ships. These enormous ships, which are many miles in diameter, can create cities within protective bubbles. Similar cities of Light already exist over, in and under the vast oceans of the planet. The bubbles are held steady by beams and energy vortexes directed to this planet from off the planet by means of way stations.[4] Such cities would be used in emergency situations until Earth becomes sufficiently stabilized or until chemical, radioactive or atmospheric pollution has subsided.

The Photon Belt

Over the past few years much discussion has occurred, both verbal and written, on the subject of the photon belt. The main concern seems to stem from the uncertainty of the experience. Is it something to be anxious about or is it a scheme to make José Argüelles[5] rich and famous?

Scientists have been monitoring photon particles for some time. The photon beam gained world recognition in the sixties when information was presented by a German scientist named Hesse. He suggested that this solar system is a part of a larger system of stars revolving around Alcyone, which is the brightest star in the Pleiades constellation. It takes Earth's sun approximately 24,000 years to complete one revolution around Alcyone. Hesse further stated that the sun passes through the photon belt twice during each 24,000-year revolution and that Earth is in position to pass through it at this time.

Scientists continue to track beams that indicate the photon belt does exist. In 1991 NASA's Atlantis shuttle studied high-energy gamma ray beams after their instruments on satellites detected the photon belt. Scientists say that photon particles affect the ratio of oxygen to carbon dioxide, which obviously would affect all life on the planet. There is speculation that if the sun passes through the belt before Earth does, there will appear to be a rain of stars. As Earth travels through the photon belt, the charged particles in the beam will affect the atmosphere. The consensus is that Earth will experience about three and a half days of darkness, and during that time no appliances will function nor will any energy production be possible. After that time new technology will have to be invented.

At present there is much panicky conversation about storing supplies, food and water for survival as well as about where groups should gather for the occasion. It is important to understand that this period of time is not meant to be a social event. During these few days a dramatic mutation will be taking place within everything on the planet and within Earth herself.

It is time for each person to create his or her own reality for this upcoming event. Use meditation periods to envision the physical self feeling relaxed, comfortably cozy and nestled, as if in a cocoon and going through the transformation into a butterfly. Each person's body will be mutating from being third-dimensional to being fifth-dimensional, so it will be advisable to eat, drink and move as little as possible, spending the time resting, sleeping and meditating.

During the greater part of those days the spirit that is each individual will be out of the physical body directing the ascension/resurrection process in the lower bodies. When the physical consciousness awakens, from time to time, awareness should remain focused on the Creator, on love, peace and the magnificence of Earth as a newly birthed star. Also, as each day passes, visualize the glorious creature that every physical being is becoming. It is also important to realize that the reason so many guides and masters from the realms of spirit are coming into people's awareness is to help during this period of transition.

The entire period will be one of great consternation for people who do not wish to change or move forward. The harder they try to maintain the status quo, the more difficult life will appear to become. The Bible refers to this as a time of "weeping, wailing and gnashing of teeth." Those with chaos in their hearts will run from place to place and from person to person seeking help outside themselves, still wanting others to "fix it" for them. Their fears can only increase as they resist the incoming vibrations. When they focus on themselves, they will experience illness that encompasses them physically, mentally and emotionally. Their bodies will find it nearly impossible to adjust.

These individuals will be convinced some of the people they love are going crazy. Friends and loved ones who are on the path might begin to communicate with spirits they are unable to see. People will use telepathy and other psychic gifts, which will make others even more confused.

For some, the appearance of spacecraft and of alien beings who look different from humans will be terrifying. They will feel as though they are caught in a time warp, and no one will be able to give them a satisfactory explanation. They will be convinced a takeover of the planet is being planned. As their paranoia increases, they will see typical human-appearing parents with children who definitely do not look completely human. (I have been noticing that this is already happening in countries around the world.)

It is important to treat these people with love. Now is not the time to try to convince anyone. Loving compassion will do more to allay fears than any words that could be might uttered. Yes, many people are here to be teachers, but the most effective way to teach is by example.

These images are only probable realities. There is no need for a disaster of any magnitude if humanity desires to move forward with Earth in her ascension. But there is an absolute necessity to stop any fear-based thoughts regarding the possible futures. Those who are able to create the reality of a smooth transition should meditate on and visualize this daily, alone or in groups. All imaging of a best-case scenario outcome will produce great benefits for the entire planet.

Raising Vibrations

A planetary ascension can take place only after the inhabitants collectively raise their vibrations. Thus, the process begins on an individual basis and as a result of a gradual awakening. The first step involves changing the way people view their experiences and how they react to those situations. In the third dimension this is the area of influence that affects the mental body on the lower mental plane.

As humans become more open in their thinking, they automatically become less judgmental, which leads to being more accepting and unconditionally loving. That is not easy in a world in which everything is judged good or bad, right or wrong. It is human nature to belittle others in an attempt to appear superior: "Look what they're doing. I would never do anything as terrible as that." A feeling of superiority carries over into jokes which derive their humor from ridiculing a particular race, religion, sex, nationality or other category.

The more a person can control his "monkey brain" so that it no longer flits from one subject to the next, the more quickly he will progress. (It has been noted that the average person spends about eighty percent of his thinking time in the past, fretting over what happened and regretting what might have been. Another eighteen percent of the time, the mind is in the future, worrying about events that have not even happened and might never happen. Only about two percent of most people's waking moments are spent in the now. Anyone who has difficulty believing this might want to keep track of his or her thoughts for the next several days. It will be quite revealing.)

That is why everyone should be spending some time each day in meditation. It stills the mind and in so doing allows the rest of the body to function better. Studies on the benefits of meditation have been carried out over the past thirty years and they all have reached the same con-

HEALING OLD HURTS

(You will need a pen and paper, matches, an ashtray, a flower seed or seeds, and if it is winter, an empty flower pot.)

Sit quietly. Breathe gently and relax your entire body.

Try to remember the situations in the past that hurt you the most and are still unresolved. Usually, they are patterns of behavior perpetrated by parents, siblings, relatives and teachers — all those who served as role models — but it could just as easily be a former husband or wife or even a present partner. The situation became a problem when you sensed you were helpless to respond the way you wanted to because you felt intimidated. Instead, you acted as though it did not matter and eventually as though it never had occurred.

After thinking back to a situation or several incidents, jot down a key phrase to describe each experience. Perhaps you would want to explore all your feelings on paper because you have never really examined them before.

clusions: meditation not only lowers blood pressure and stress levels but it also reverses the aging process. People who meditate live longer and have a better quality of life.

As a person begins to create a more loving, less stressful life, his mental body rises up from the denser subplanes. The subatomic particles that make up this body are actually able to carry more Light. The entire

When you have finished writing, crumple the paper into an ashtray and burn it until nothing remains but ashes. Visualize the process of transformation as those hurts and old wounds go up in smoke.

Now those old injuries are no longer in the same form. They have been transmuted by fire. You are now ready to make something good out of a painful and frustrating situation.

If it is warm outside, take the ashes and dig a hole the proper depth for your flower seed(s). Place the ashes in the bottom of the hole and plant the seed. You may prefer to buy a young plant. Lovingly place the seed or plant in the soil, knowing you have changed the negative energy of the past into a thing of beauty for the future. (If it is winter, you can use a pot and do the same procedure indoors.)

Water the soil. Send love to your seeds and soil daily. Believe your life and health will be different from that moment on because you have released the negativity and hurts you have been hanging onto for so long.

mental body begins to radiate a sunshine-yellow glow; it is becoming the sun. Individual actions allow the mental body to move from the lower stratum of the mental plane and progress higher and higher. The sparkling Light penetrates all the way through to the physical body and influences it positively.

In conjunction with controlling his thoughts, a person should become aware of his emotions. That will not be too difficult, for many people have felt a lot like Jekyll and Hyde lately — happy one minute, crying the next, lonely the next and then angry or even insanely optimistic. Some people fear they are regressing to their teen years when hormones were running their lives.

The depth of some of emotions is shocking, because for years it was so easy to bury the hurt and anger deep within the emotional body until there was no longer any awareness that those feelings existed. Now the increased vibrations are churning the waters of the emotional body until all that hidden debris works its way to the surface. This process can also cause a lot of aches and pains in places where there has never been a problem in the past.

Old emotions can be fatal! Bitterness, anger and hate can cause life-threatening illnesses, so it is important to get rid of the hurts. One of the most effective ways to rid the self of deep-seated resentments is through transmutation. The process called "Healing Old Hurts" can be extremely effective.

Now is the time for people to start monitoring their emotions and come to the awareness that no one on the outside can hurt their feelings. It is only a person's ego and self-image that feel the pain, embarrassment or lack of self-worth. It is time for people to learn to see themselves as sparks of the Divine. There is one affirmation that can be used daily because it encompasses all others:

"I AM that I AM, DIVINE PERFECTION."

This is a wonderful way to begin the morning and it can be used throughout the day, anytime feelings of imperfection arise. This powerful phrase cancels negative thoughts and self-doubt.

Once a person begins to rule his or her emotions rather than allowing them to be in charge, life becomes happier almost instantly. When there is nothing to worry about and nothing to feel bad about, it becomes possible to be like advanced yogis and masters who giggle at the joy of life. The more time individuals spend in joy, the more quickly their atoms fill with Light. The Light particles that fill the mental and emotional bodies influence the amount of Light the etheric and physical bodies can contain.

There comes a time when a person has changed so much that one organ — the eyes, for example — will become transformed so that he is able to "see" only the good in everything. His vision has moved beyond what is normally considered perfect vision. Then another organ will become perfected. These flawless organs will greatly affect the organs around them.

The next part of you to experience perfection will be a system, like the digestive system or the endocrine system. The mental, emotional and etheric/physical bodies are learning to work together as a perfect organism so patience is necessary, but once colds and headaches stop occurring, it is good to acknowledge the growing perfection by appreciating your body.

There will come a time when fifty-one percent of a body's cells have reached a higher vibration. At that instant, all the cells will fire simultaneously and be transmuted. At the present time, the etheric body is connected to the physical body via the red-colored vortex of energy at the base of the spine. Red is the densest color vibration in the spectrum. The emotional body is connected to the physical by orange energy that enters the physical body just beneath the navel. Yellow energy flows from the mental body into the physical body at the solar plexus. The color of each chakra is a higher vibration than the one beneath it because color carries its own vibrational frequency. As the cellular structure of the body functions in greater peace and love, the chakras operate at higher and higher frequencies. When all the cells of the lower bodies reach a specific vibration, they are fired simultaneously. All subatomic particles will be vibrating at the level of the heart chakra. This is the process of Ascension!

It has happened to other individuals from time to time throughout history. The most vivid example is the evidence contained in the fabric of the Shroud of Turin. The impressions on the Shroud were made at the instant when the cells of Jesus' body fired and actually burned his likeness into the material. After that moment Jesus' physical body was no longer third-dimensional.

This is a unique and historical time to be living on Earth as all inhabitants will take part in a Planetary Ascension! The planet and humanity will become one. When the population has reached critical mass by raising their vibrations and becoming spirit-conscious or Christed,[6] the remainder of the inhabitants and the planet will transform instantly!

What unbelievable joy! Is it any wonder thousands of "unwanted" babies are flooding the planet? Everyone who possibly can wants to take part in the experience. There is no need to question why so many spacecraft are visiting Earth from distant planetary systems. How special it is to be one of those chosen to lead the rest of humanity by showing them the way. There are not many worlds or many beings who will ever have such an opportunity, and those who have that chance now have waited eons for it.

Now is the time for each person to remember that he or she has awakened ahead of the great majority and is, therefore, one of the teachers, one of the healers here to help birth the planet. Those involved in the process of midwifing are awakening their god-selves. Unfathomable numbers of souls have incarnated on Earth since the beginning, so all could not be present at this time; there simply is not enough space. Those who are here now are considered fortunate by all those watching from the different dimensions. This is some indication of how extraordinary these times are. Relax and enjoy the ride. It is just going to get better.

The following meditation was designed to help in the process of ascension.

MEDITATION INCREASING VIBRATIONS IN THE PRIMARY AURIC FIELD

Put yourself in a relaxed, meditative state. You might want to have soothing music in the background. Make certain you will not be disturbed. It is possible to make your own audio recording of this meditation so that you will not have to refer to the book for the steps; nothing is more relaxing and healing than the soothing sound of your own voice.

1. Imagine yourself lying on a beautiful beach by the ocean. Hear the rhythmic waves gently washing the shore. The sand warms your back. A soft breeze cools you. Become aware of your yellow mental body. It is larger than your physical body and is made up of lines like acupuncture meridians. There is also a more subtle field of energy that is a part of this mental body and extends beyond it, forming a spherical shape. You are encased in the protective energy of the mental body. All around the outside edge of this energy field is very fine, highly vibrating energy. Like the shell of an egg, it is even greater protection which, and it does not allow anything of a denser nature to penetrate. This protection can be weakened or damaged by drug use whether legal or illegal.

Now imagine the sphere of the sun slowly coming down into your solar plexus (the upside down V under your sternum where your ribs separate). Feel its warmth. Concentrate on radiating the sun's energy in every direction so it completely fills your mental body and then the sphere beyond it. Look for any dark areas in the field where the golden rays do not penetrate or cannot flow. Bombard those areas with golden Light. Feel the sun's warmth flowing in these areas once again. The mental body is now radiant with sunshine-yellow rays.

2. The life-giving force in all creation is love. Your emotional body heals and evolves through love. It is now time to fill your emotional body with the maximum amount of love. This body should be filled with and should radiate all the colors of the rainbow. When you are angry or sad or disappointed, these colors become muddied and dark. Concentrate now on bringing a large sphere of ruby, pink-violet loving energy into the heart center of your emotional body. Fill your heart, your chest and then your whole body. Look to see that all the colors are pure and that no blockages remain. Keep radiating the love farther and farther, for this less dense body can extend quite an extraordinary distance from your physical body. Remember, the supply of love in the universe is infinite.

   After your body has absorbed as much loving energy as it can, you might wish to beam loving rays to your family and friends, to the neighborhood, the country and the world. It is a wonderful exercise to do at least daily. You can help Earth cleanse her aura through this process as well.

3. The next body is the etheric body. This body is a replica of the physical body, only it is less dense. It has clearly defined meridians of energy. You are going to use two rays for the etheric body. The first is the healing ray of Earth, an elec-

tric blue. All the masters have used Earth's ray in their healing work. Bring this ray up from the center of Earth
through your feet and hands. Let it slowly rise up through
the rest of your body and exit your head at the crown
chakra. See your etheric body becoming electric blue. Examine it with your inner sight to be sure there are no breaks
or blocks in the flow of energy. Allow this blue energy to
flow from your crown chakra far into space as Earth's gift
to the universe.

The second energy ray required by the etheric body is called
the Christ energy. (Christ energy does not refer to "Jesus
energy" but to the highest vibrational frequency in this
local universe. Jesus did not have this energy until he
became the Christ; you will unite with this energy when
you attain your Christhood, or become Christed.[6]) Christ
energy looks like sunlight sparkling on snow, like diamonds
in the sun. Bring the energy of the universe into your
crown chakra. It moves down your body, lighting up the
space within every atom of your being. Ask that your bodies be able to absorb the maximum amount of Christ energy
or as it is called in other traditions, prana or chi. Let its
light flow out of your hands and feet and down into the
Earth Mother to nourish her. You have now become a river
of flowing energies. One flow grounds you into the Earth
while the other renews your connection with the universe.

(It is important to understand that pain and illness are
always produced by energy that has become stuck. When
you check daily to see that your rivers of energy are flowing,
you take a major step toward ridding yourself of pain and
moving into perfect health. In the future, humanity will no
longer require food but will be sustained by Christ energy.)

Now concentrate on the energy flowing along your spine
and radiating out on either side of it. Also imagine the

reservoir of the spleen being filled to capacity with this energy. Next, join the etheric and physical bodies together and let the energies all flow into the physical body. See the physical spine and central nervous system being energized and the physical spleen being filled. (The reason the medical profession has not yet discovered a use for the spleen is that it is the body's reservoir of Christ energy.)

4. The next step is to align your mental, emotional, etheric and physical bodies. When you feel they are integrated, bond them together with a golden laser beam. The first golden beam comes down through your crown chakra, moves down your spine and extends beyond your feet. The second beam enters your left arm at heart level and leaves through your right arm. The third beam enters your heart through the chest wall at heart level and exits out the back. Now the bodies are perfectly synchronized with one another. When you are centered, balanced and in life's river of energy, you will no longer become tired. The supply is always here if you are open to it.

Hint: if you are feeling mentally scattered, unfocused, tired or ungrounded and do not have time or the proper setting to do this meditation, here is a quick technique. Remember how babies sigh after a hard cry? I call it a "hitched sigh." The deep inhalation is not smooth but rather jerky and the exhale is long and smooth. Try to recall the memory of this breath. "Break" the inhalation at least three times. If you could hear your breath, it would sound like this: (inhale) hih, hih, hih, hih . . . (exhale) . . . s-i-g-h. Now all the bodies are in alignment. This is a wondrous technique for releasing both mental and physical rigidity. It works well to reduce stress in all situations but especially problems such as Chronic Fatigue Syndrome and Epstein Barr.

It is time to remember that life on this planet has been an experiment. Many souls created bodies to experience density and the material world; they chose to investigate separation and duality. Now they are on the journey home. The most difficult work is behind and the glorious work lies ahead. The separation ends as people awaken to their oneness with All That Is — not just here, not just now, but everywhere and for all time. The more each can identify with his or her individual uniqueness, the more it is possible to appreciate being totally one. Individuals are really Sparks of the Creator who is the Source of all Light: "I and my Father are One" or, in New Thought, "I Am one with Source." This is all very beautiful and very esoteric but it is time to learn the details of personal ascension.

NOTES

1. Pranic breathing utilizes Chi, Qi or universal energy in yoga-style breathing.

2. Holotropic Breathwork is a method or approach to self-exploration originated by Stanislaus Grof, M.D.

3. Every dimension is further divided into seven subplanes.

4. Way stations are artificially created platforms in space that serve many functions.

5. Argüelles, present-day expert on the Mayan calendar, first spread the word among the New Age community that passing through the Belt would result in the end of Earth's technology as we know it.

6. "Christed" refers to the act of becoming a Christ. Jesus' life exemplified how to attain this lofty goal. It is not necessary to die to become Christed. This universe operates on and through Christ energy.

Ascension/Resurrection

The physical man hath a body with a heart.
The spiritual man hath a heart with a body.
The Lords of Light protect and aid one on the path
who carrieth on the work of the Light.

Ann Ree Colton

Ascension is one of the most misunderstood concepts in the world today. In the early Greek language, there was only one word for both ascension and resurrection; they meant the same thing. According to Webster's New Universal Unabridged Dictionary, "Ascension" is the process of rising up, specifically, "the bodily ascent of Jesus into Heaven" while "resurrection" is "a rising from the dead."

Aquarians who discuss New Thought believe resurrection involves a complete transformation. They refer to resurrection/ascension as a repatterning of the frequency or vibrational rates of the atoms that make up the body; the body is enlivened. In the Bible, Daniel 12:3 says that the "resurrected will shine like stars."[1] Paul indicated in his letters to the Corinthians that the people who knew Jesus believed in his resurrection because of his bright appearance after the crucifixion and not, as the modern Church stresses, because they heard anything or saw that the tomb was empty. It is important to understand that Jesus went through such a dramatic change from death to life so that humanity would be convinced that such a transformation was and is possible for everyone.

Jesus is not the only man the Bible mentions as having ascended. It also tells of Enoch's ascension in Genesis and of Elijah's in Kings II. It is also interesting to note that all major religions tell, in their histories and mythologies, of leaders who endured deaths similar to the crucifixion of Jesus. Following their deaths, these leaders were resurrected and, in front of many believers, ascended. Three examples are Buddha, Krishna and Kukulkan.

Only a few people in Earth's history have been able to ascend, because ascension has meant mastery over all of the lower bodies. Only then is it possible to live outside the influence of duality. It is said that the masters of the East wear robes of white that never get dirty; they are in such a state of perfection that nothing imperfect can approach them.

Archeologists have found many different classifications of early humans such as Cro-Magnon, Neanderthal and so on, but they have never found a missing link between each of the different categories. Why is that? It will be learned that at a certain point in development, a mutation took place throughout the species and the human suddenly transformed into the next level or stage of evolvement. Humanity is once again at that critical juncture. More and more people are awakening to their Godhood. The next evolutionary step will be moving from "hu-man" to "God-man." Once again, it will be impossible to discover the missing link.

It is a time when humanity is recognizing that the Creator is within every individual. As the human species moves up to the next spiral, most people on the planet will be members of a new root race. Before the firing of the cells takes place so that the mutation can occur, several steps must be taken; this process has already begun.

Personal Changes

One of the greatest changes to occur is that each individual is awakening from a limited framework of consciousness. Instead of using only ten percent of his or her brain capacity, the human will be able to access one hundred percent of the brain's capabilities. Using even thirty-five or fifty percent of the brain dramatically increases awareness. The senses are heightened as the brain becomes capable of interpreting all sensory information. Naturally, data are easily stored and retained. Both halves of the brain will be fully integrated and balanced. (Beings are already coming into infant physical bodies having accomplished this.) There will be increased receptivity and perception. People will start remembering or have flashbacks to past lives. Individuals will grow in an awareness of what others are thinking and of how animals are feeling. People will start to recognize when their plants are sick or feeling neglected.

Think of what humans will be able to see when they are using ninety-five percent more of their visual capacity! In the future human eyes will become larger and more symmetrical. At the moment most people cannot see into the infrared or ultraviolet spectrum, but that will change rapidly. In the beginning it is useful to remember that it is easier to see into the ultraviolet range after dark, while seeing people's auras is easiest at dusk when the eye is switching from the use of rods to cones. Individuals who see spirits or angelic beings are simply using more of their visual capacity than is the average human.

All the senses are becoming keener, including taste, touch and hearing. No longer will people be able to tolerate extremely loud music. When awareness is expanded through meditation by becoming one with All That Is, it becom ; possible to 1 ?ar the music of the spheres. More and more New Agers are becoming extremely sensitive to aromas, which is one of the reasons healing with flower essences has become so popular.

Discovering Wellness

At the moment most people are aware only of their physical bodies, but with expanded awareness, they will also work consciously with their mental, emotional, etheric and other bodies. These other bodies are aware of the physical body, although it is not aware of them. A mantra suggested by Italian psychiatrist Dr. Roberto Assagioli can help to avoid identifying with the physical body: "I have a thinking body, but it is not me. I have a feeling body, but it is not me. I have a physical/etheric body, but it is not me. I use these. I *am* the soul."

Once people awaken from their present limited thinking, they will realize their bodies have never descended from perfection; they will see the illusion of past limited thinking and begin recreating their perfect selves. Most illness originates in the emotional body or the mental body. From there it goes into *(infects)* the etheric body. The last body to become ill is the physical body. Several doctors in countries such as India have developed cameras that photograph the aura and can detect a pregnancy minutes after conception and breast tumors that would not show up on a mammogram until six months later.

As people become emotionally healthier and more spiritually attuned, it will be easier to be totally healed and to remain in perfect health. It is important to remember that healing the body is one thing, but if the emotional, mental and spiritual problems that caused the illness are not resolved, the disease will recur. The most difficult challenge is to separate from the collective unconscious. When television ads are filled with headache remedies, hemorrhoid ointments and anti-gray hair coloring products, it is very difficult to convince the brain that the body of which it is part is an exception to the illness and aging process. The best way to do that is to send love to the body and to know that with perfected thinking, it will become perfect.

Many individuals on their path are trying to treat their physical bodies better than they ever have before in this lifetime, yet they suffer from aches, pains, flu and various symptoms for which no doctor can determine a cause. The good news is that physical symptoms are an indication that the body's vibrational level is increasing. The higher vibrations actually shake old stagnant energy out of the organs, muscles and tissues just like a dog shaking off water. Even though these high vibrations are causing more aches and pains now, eventually all the discomfort will disappear. Any kind of bodywork such as massage or energy therapy can be very helpful in moving the stuck energy out of the body more quickly.

All the physical bodies are being restructured at a cellular level while the other bodies are changing vibrationally. It is now possible to completely clear many problems that doctors have labeled chronic. I have witnessed miracles happening in cases of major illnesses from multiple sclerosis to rheumatoid arthritis, and everything in between. I know many people who have been severely limited, physically and mentally for many years who will become perfect within the next five to seven years. They have chosen lives of extreme pain or limitation so they might clear the karmic slate of all past life injustices which they committed against others. It must be remembered that these are very highly evolved souls. Using telepathy with those who cannot speak can reveal some interesting stories.

Physical Symptoms Common to the Ascension Process

There are quite a number of physical changes occurring in human bodies because the species is evolving. Those who have not yet been affected can expect to notice symptoms in the near future.

1. Ringing in the ears
   a. Messages are actually being sent in tonal patterns.
   b. People are becoming aware of the sounds of individual

organs. In the future, it will be possible to detect if the heart or gall bladder or liver is stressed because they will be out of harmony with the rest of the body's tones.

   c. People are becoming more sensitive to the electronic waves and frequencies which penetrate most areas of the globe. These high-pitched sounds can become very loud and distracting at times.

2. Heart palpitations occur as the heart restructures in alignment with a higher vibration. The muscles of the heart have always been striated vertically, as are all organs that are involuntary. Recently more and more of the heart's muscles are becoming striated horizontally, which means that in the future, people will be responsible for the action of their hearts. Advanced yogis always know how to control their hearts and other organs.

3. A change in eyesight

   a. Blurring of vision occurs as the eyes restructure.

   b. People think they see someone beyond their range of vision, just over their shoulder. In truth, they are seeing into another dimension and actually seeing an etheric being or spirit.

   c. Some individuals see waterfalls of light and halos around electric lights. This is terrifying for those who know someone with glaucoma, but the truth is they are beginning to see into other dimensions. In the beginning people seldom see straight ahead into other planes. Instead, they see into other planes peripherally, or from the side.

   d. Many people, especially those in their twenties and younger, see the colorful auras around everyone and everything.

4. Hot and cold flashes regardless of age and gender, are the result of metabolic changes. This unpleasantness can be greatly alleviated by rapping gently below the notch in the throat at the

thymus gland. People also find it helpful to request that their guides regulate their metabolism while they are sleeping.

5. Experiencing chills throughout the body occurs when someone is imparting information. This is the new way the body has chosen to let individuals become informed of their own truth. It also allows a person to adjust the frequency of his or her own vibration to that of another, which becomes increasingly important as the masters come here to teach humanity.

6. Difficulty with memory sometimes occurs, leading people to wonder if they are losing their minds, because they seem to be forgetting more information than they are remembering. This is happening because useless data are being deleted from individual memory banks, especially the untruths programmed during school years. It allows areas of the brain to be used more efficiently.

7. A sense of loss and a feeling of being overwhelmed with sadness can fill the emotions, often with good reason. Lifelong friends and even family might have become distant. It is increasingly difficult to find something in common. Serious illness is affecting individuals or their loved ones. Many people are losing their jobs and homes. So much is changing in such a short time. This is not punishment; it is happening so that people will move into the areas of service they came into this lifetime to perform.

8. Food cravings occur, especially for sweets. It is comforting to know that meditation and psychic work use far more of the brain's blood sugar than do normal activities. Physical bodies require far less food than most people think they do, but they require greater amounts of purified water. Fewer medications, drugs, hormones and supplements are needed now, and many people are aware of an increasing sensitivity to artificial prod-

ucts. Drugs, alcohol, food and sex mask what must be faced in life now.

All these symptoms seem to come and go along with the aches and pains as old energy blocks work their way to the surface.

Life Changes

One of the first and most important aspects of moving into the fifth dimension is to recognize that nothing is forever. Never before in Earth's history has humanity experienced such continuous change. In the past, entire families lived in one town, children grew up knowing that their mothers were at home and their grandparents were nearby. Fathers worked at one job. Parents stayed together because it was expected that they would.

Now the future is filled with uncertainty. It is a lesson in learning to trust. It hardly pays to make elaborate plans any more because there will undoubtedly be changes, but when people trust that these changes are occurring for the highest good of all, life seems more like a package full of hidden surprises.

Many people find they can no longer read daily newspapers or watch the news on television, for there is simply too much emphasis on the negative. New Agers are more interested in positive events. A glance at the nonfiction bestseller list or at the books people are reading reveals a surprising amount of material that reflects new thinking and the necessity of taking personal responsibility.

Canceling the Eve Syndrome

Women's lives are reflecting interesting and positive changes. In the not-too-distant future, women will no longer suffer from PMS or have pain during childbirth. The exciting news is that this is already happening. Reports I hear from women in the West say that the majority of young mothers are giving birth after only one or two major contractions;

they seldom spend days in labor as their mothers did.

Much of the pain women experience dates back to the beginning of Judeo-Christian teachings when the belief was perpetrated that Eve was responsible for all human suffering. All women were second-class citizens from that time on.

The plight of women became even worse several hundred years ago when the Catholic Church began prohibiting women who were giving birth from having a midwife present to help them. The Church said women had to suffer because they were carrying with them the guilt of Eve. It got to the point where they could not even brew a cup of tea for fear of being branded a witch.

Centuries of negative thought forms surrounding women formed the basis for their collective unconscious. Pain and suffering during a woman's cycle became a sort of collective self-punishment. But now women are rapidly changing their consciousnesses and, therefore, their realities. Soon it will be accepted that the "fall" of humanity had nothing to do with Eve but rather with a disengaging by all humanity from continuous conscious connection with their higher selves and the Creator.

To Leave or Not to Leave the Physical Body

Earth's population is coming of age. People are beginning to realize that the old paradigms no longer work, including illness, aging and death. People are starting to believe that the necessity of growing old is an illusion and that an even more mistaken belief is the idea that they must get sick in order to die. "Primitive" or aboriginal peoples know it is possible to choose a specific time to leave the physical body. When the decision has been made, the spirit is simply withdrawn. With the spirit gone, the physical body's processes slow and finally stop. Following that, the etheric body begins to disintegrate.

New beliefs change reality. It is now possible to go beyond choosing the moment of death by joining the company of those who are not planning to die at all — ever again. All of the ascended masters have their bodies. Jesus has continued to appear from time to time on the physical plane in a body that is over two thousand years old. The emerging concept is that humans will change their third-dimensional bodies to fifth-dimensional. The soul creates a body from the energy matrix for Earth humans. It is this Adam Kadmon pattern which is the spiritual matrix, or blueprint of Light from which Adamic man is created. This blueprint is always a part of every human and it is the template of perfection. It is what all humanity is growing into.

I can hear people muttering to themselves right now, thinking, "If I were going to keep a body for the next several thousand years, why would I have chosen this one?" The truth is, if people could see themselves in all their glorious perfection, they would be amazed at how breathtakingly beautiful they are.

Scientists have been trying to tell people that they are more than 99% space. That is because the body is made up of atoms, which are mostly space. What makes people appear solid is that the energy vibration has slowed down dramatically. As humanity moves toward ascension, and as the increased energy continues to bombard Earth, the atoms that make up people's bodies are absorbing more Light. That is what causes a radiant glow to emanate from the skin, eyes, teeth and hair.

Upgrading Energy

There are a few last words on energy that are important. It is critical to upgrade the energy of all electronic appliances. People's energies are rapidly accelerating, especially if they are working on themselves. Therefore, it becomes necessary to be surrounded by machines that are compatible with their increasing vibrations. People are burning out motors at an alarming rate. Those who work on computers are experiencing strange reactions from their machines.

Many people's energies are becoming so high that they also knock out street lights as they pass. I was recently told about a group of ten healers who had been invited by the staff of a particular hospital to demonstrate their skills to the doctors. As the ten healers walked through the entrance of the hospital at the same time, all the electrical circuits in the hospital blew. While technicians worked with auxiliary power, the healers worked to make their energy compatible with that of the equipment in the hospital. People who forget to upgrade their appliances periodically find that healing techniques like Reiki work well to bring their equipment back to life and extend it just a little longer.

Who Am "I"?

People very subtly create their world with "I AM" statements. The Bible tells the reader that "I AM" is the name of God. "I AM that I AM" is a powerful statement, for it affirms the God-self by invoking the unlimited power of the Creator and directing it into every area of life. It is vital to pay attention to all "I am" phrases. Saying, "I am so sick," "I am tired," "I am broke," and so on adds tremendous energy to those statements and creates a negative reality. It also connects the speaker through the collective unconscious to the millions living in poverty. Instead, such verbalized thoughts can be started with, "I am aware . . . , " "I choose . . . ," or "I know . . . ."

At this juncture in my ascension process, I am consciously trying to think of and refer to my body as "*not* me." For example, I think that "This body is tired now. It should go to bed." This sounds very strange at first but that indicates how skewed traditional thinking is. This practice helps to remind me that I am spirit and that my physical body is only one of my many aspects, like an outfit I have chosen to wear.

Even though most people will want to change their thinking about who they are, as opposed to who their bodies are, the physical body is extremely important and it is time to listen lovingly to it. If the body feels tired, give it more rest. Small children need a lot of rest while their bodies are growing and undergoing such remarkable changes; the same is true for all human bodies at this time.

The greatest changes begin to occur when a person can visualize his body as returning to perfection. It will then begin to glow with living Light. A beautiful aura will fill the atmosphere around the body, and its radiance will become as brilliant as an exquisite diamond. This is the true body humans were meant to exhibit. Such a magnificent body is so in harmony with cosmic love that no virus or decay can find a space to invade. The atoms and cells are filled with Light and love. When the body is in such a state, it could be crucified hundreds of times and still be triumphant, for it is continually and eternally resurrected. Just as the potential of the giant oak tree lies within the tiny acorn, so the incredible, vast Christ lies within every human being.

The human was designed with enormous care. Many advanced biologists and geneticists worked diligently over time to create humanity. Individual spirits specifically and precisely constructed perfect bodies for this particular mission. The human body is still in its outer wrapping, giving only a hint of its contents, but the season is fast approaching when humans will be able to open the package and discover their true beauty, beauty that has never been seen in a mirror. Each individual must unwrap his own gift and awaken to reconnect with his higher self in this lifetime. Once that has been done, the Light will be shared throughout the planet.

The Guru Within

People frequently ask me when their personal gurus will appear. They would prefer to leave their hectic lives and sit at their masters' feet for the next ten years. Unfortunately for them, the days of gurus, priests and shamans is rapidly approaching an end. Buddha told this to his followers and the Bible says the same thing: "You do not need anyone to teach you." Everyone already knows how to access the perfect body, the perfect partner, the perfect job or the perfect knowledge. The only place to find it and all other great truths is within. Others will come forward to be helpers, but each person's greatest instruction from now on will come from his or her higher self.

It is important to use discretion when attending workshops or reading books and to observe how teachers present not only the information but themselves. In the past, the priests and shamans always reserved the highest secrets for themselves, standing apart from their chelas (students). Now is the time to share all information. The teacher must lovingly set the example. It is the time for the teacher to *be* love.

A drop of water removed from the ocean has very little value, but as a part of the ocean it is a powerful force. The same principle applies to love. Every little act of kindness, every loving glance or touch, every reassuring word becomes a part of the vast ocean of cosmic love, instantly connecting the doer with that tremendous force for good in the universe. As a person exists more and more in oneness with cosmic love, the good he or she can do increases exponentially, for everyone is teaching others by who he is and who he is becoming.

As more and more people align themselves consciously with this pure energy, Earth will become Heaven. That is what Earth was meant to be. It is important to remember that every atom, cell, plant, human, planet, star or universe has one cohesive force and that is love. Earth is meant to be the jewel of this solar system. Humanity can love Mother Earth into perfection and themselves along with her.

Purpose

Every being in every Universe has two requirements: continuous learning and service to others. The idea of performing some kind of service often seems impossible to people because their lives are so busy as it is. But then people discover that their realities change once they have survived a natural disaster or suffered a serious illness or been through a near-death experience. They arrive at the realization that all are one; when one person has a problem, it affects everyone. Survivors learn to make time in their routines to do something extra for others. They find they need to be serving others and their service not only brings them tremendous rewards but also helps them to grow. It teaches them that greater happiness comes from giving than from receiving. A person's first criterion in deciding what kind of service to perform should be to do something in a field he loves. There must be passion.

All these eons of time, humans have been concerned with survival. Now the time has come when they can do what they love doing and get paid for it too. Nothing anyone has done in this lifetime, no experience anyone has ever had will be wasted. Every lesson and each experience was chosen in preparation for this time. Many people are not yet in a job they love, but by doing service in that area, they can gain the experience to make the changeover in careers. I have heard many beautiful stories about how people came to be working at what they love to do by first being of service.

Recently I met a man who as a child had had the bones in his feet broken and reset to form an arch. According to his story, he was in such pain as an adult that he could not stand on his feet for more than five minutes. To gain relief, he designed orthotics for himself and discovered a revolutionary idea which is now helping hundreds of people to feel better and to be on their feet with less pain. And, I might add, he is making a ton of money!

Let Your Light Shine

People in service are called Lightworkers because their appearance is becoming brighter and brighter. One of the ways a person can become aware of his own brightness is to pay attention on a visit to a crowded supermarket, department store or any place where there are lots of children. They stare at people whose Light is unusually bright.

At those times when life is flowing well and a person is feeling in harmony and expansive, the atoms of the body are able to absorb increasingly more Light. Eventually the body's cells reach critical mass of Light containment. It will take most people a little longer than it took Jesus because he spent his whole life preparing to become Christed, but others have probably just arrived at the idea that this possibility exists for them. The churches most people attended as children did not exactly prepare them to become Christs; in fact, they did just the opposite by trying to maintain the separation between God and humans.

The Source, the Creator, God — all are names for Divine Love Energy that expresses Itself in Light. It is time for people to reprogram their thinking to accept that the walls, chairs and floors that are everywhere and that seem so dense are made up of that same divine energy and therefore, are made of Light. Thought alone has densified them to the point of their becoming solid. It is possible to imagine the molecular structure of everything as vibrating faster and containing more space and to visualize the material world as loving, moving energy and particles of Light.

ASCENSION WITH EASE

The energy bombarding Earth is also creating havoc with human bodies. Flu-like symptoms, aches, feeling hot or cold, toxicity, congestion and anxiety mean that all those well-hidden emotions are coming to the surface to be dealt with. What can be done?

1. *Surrender* to the process and progress will be faster.

2. *Food.* Watch your diet: eat lighter foods, cut out junk food,

bless your food and fill it with Light; fast to give your digestive organs a deserved break.

3. *Rest.* Take a time-out when your body tells you it is tired. Your body is growing in many ways and needs extra rest just as a child's body does.

4. *Bathe* with minerals and salts in the presence of crystals and candles to help yourself change your pace or unwind from a hectic day.

5. *Meditate.* After years of research, it has been proven that meditation reduces stress — mental, emotional and physical. It also heals and rejuvenates the body.

6. *Laugh.* Laughter is great medicine, as Norman Cousins proved. Learn to see the humor in most all situations. Have you seen yogis or the Dalai Lama on television? They constantly smile and even giggle. Take yourself less seriously.

7. *Forgive.* Forgiveness is the first step in healing. You can never clear toxins or heal an illness in your body if you are holding a grudge. No unresolved fight or bitter conversation of the past is worth dying for.

8. *Tears.* Cry if you want to. When babies are in frustrating situations, they become increasingly tense and rigid. Finally, they cry and release all stress. It is important to really cry, not just leak.

9. *Exercise your spine.* An inflexible spine is an indication of an inflexible mind.

10. *Love, sing and rejoice* constantly. If you don't awaken happy, excited and filled with anticipation, you are not following this list.

Release and Go with the Flow

People are reacting strangely to the events in their lives. I know people who hate their jobs and say they would do anything to be free from that situation but do not know how to make a change. At a subconscious level, they are asking to be released but then when their boss fires them, they are sick with remorse. They do not seem to understand that they created the situation for themselves on another level.

I counsel many people who detest their spouses and want desperately to be out of their marriages. However, when the spouses announce they have found new loves and are leaving, their partners are devastated. What is wrong? These people have asked their higher selves for change and yet when it comes, they are angry and filled with resentment. It is imperative that people realize that they are creating every circumstance they need to go forward in their lives. It is also important to understand on a deep level that every change is for the best.

People would do well to relax and enjoy life. It is time to allow other people to solve their own problems rather than feeling the need to play the role of peacekeeper. Others cannot learn their lessons unless there is an absence of interference. Not long ago I was walking on a desert path with a woman I had just met. At one point, she tried to break off the pad of a cactus so "other people might not scratch their legs on it." I knew immediately she was overly caring; she was trying to make the situation perfect for others. That is no longer advisable. If someone needs to learn not to walk so close to a cactus, then so be it. Now is the time when people need to distance themselves from getting caught up in solving other people's problems. If there is trouble in a relationship, it is helpful to stand outside the circle or look down from above and watch the action. A different perspective will often reveal a new solution. A word of warning: friends and relatives are shocked when they find they can no longer entangle a person in their problems, and they try desperately to get the former personality back.

Eighty percent of people's dilemmas would immediately disappear if they could forget all references to the past. Isn't that amazing? What a person did at another time, how he reacted last week or even fifty years ago was the best way he knew to act at the time. No one is to blame. Everyone is to be forgiven. Each person is attracting all the experiences he needs for the lessons he has wanted to learn. Everyone in a person's life mirrors the feelings that person has for himself. As people strive for perfection, they become far more impatient with themselves for catching a cold or losing control of their emotions. It is very natural to have periods of doubt, and no one is immune to that. Instead of berating themselves, it would be better if they were to ask their guides for help, eat a hot fudge sundae, sit in a bubble bath or take the afternoon off to enjoy something they have wanted to do for a long time.

Little by little, feelings of happiness begin to occur for no reason. People want to sing or raise their arms up to the sky and say, "Thank you, God!" These moments of bliss start to arise more frequently and to last longer each time. Inner radiance glows from every pore. When they walk, their feet barely touch the ground. They begin to attract others like themselves, friends they have been looking for all their lives, and instead of one, there will be dozens. It no longer takes years to get to know them, for they are from the same soul group and each will recognize the other immediately. The amusing thing to me is that they do not look the same as I remember them — before they chose their present bodies — but I recognize them by their vibrations.

Past Lives: Pressures and Processing

Past lifetimes that are relevant to this lifetime are now coming into awareness for many. They can come in the form of day dreams or night dreams, during meditations or simply as feelings of deja vu. (My guides now interpret my dreams and I am getting so much more out of them than the obvious interpretation provided by my training or limited understanding; other people's guides might do the same.) Dreams often let people know that they are stuck in a situation by showing them a past life that involved a similar circumstance; sometimes the players are still the same. Rather than feeling frustrated about being unable to determine a meaning, it is best to ask before sleeping the following night that the information be presented in a different way, which usually happens whether it is asked for or not. At this time avoiding additional pressure is paramount. It must be understood that it doesn't matter where a particular individual is on the path. It is not a race to see who can get there first.

In fact, it is my belief that when people think they are making little or no progress, they are accomplishing the most; it is just that advances are occurring at a far deeper level of consciousness. A lot of conscious information can feel wonderful, but working on a subconscious level without even being aware makes it an integral part of life, and that indicates real progress.

It is important to learn simply to trust the process. I recently moved from one end of the country to the other, and I knew only one person upon arrival. I do not really know why I am here or for how long, but I do know I am happier than I have ever been. Every day I meet others who have been told to move here also. All they could do was trust.

People must believe deep in their hearts that they have chosen to be here at this particular time to share the most exciting event in Earth's history. They will soon realize that the time is fast approaching when they will understand the illusion of death. (I do not intend to die in this lifetime. I can recall other lifetimes when I did not die because I could control the rate of vibration of the cells in my body, but it does take a concentrated effort to do it. Many people ask themselves why they would want to live forever in the world the way it is now, but it will not be this way for long. Soon life will be filled with joy and instant rewards.

There is a story regarding John the Divine, who wrote the Book of Revelation. He made his friends promise not to disturb him, no matter what. Then he locked himself in a room and did what he had to do. Many years later, they felt surely John was dead, probably from starvation, and wanted to give him a proper burial. When they entered his room, they found no one, not even his bones. It seems he knew the secret.

Each person who is reading this book is feeling something special, something he cannot label. It is the deep urging of the soul toward perfection. Some people have come back from the future to help Earth birth herself into the fifth dimension. Many of them will be the teachers and healers of the future. Now they are the disseminators of truth, and they will take the seeds of wisdom with them whereever they go. Some people might not work with this information for months or years, some will begin to change their lives tomorrow. It doesn't matter. Each one is on his or her own schedule.

Channeling and Authenticity

It is essential that each person recognize his or her own truth. Not all channeled information is based in truth because channelers have what is termed, in the corporate world, a glass ceiling. Many people who channel are contacting spirit beings who are not evolved or who are astral shells from the lower astral plane. The information received is only as authentic as the spirit who is contacted. How is it possible to determine if the spirits being channeled are who they say they are? They must be asked in a straight-forward way if they represent the highest good of all or if they are speaking God's truth. They will not lie when asked very direct, yes-or-no questions. Of course, total openness to the answer is necessary.

Let me give you an example. I have a acquaintance who channels an archangel and another master on an electric typewriter. The messages are garbled and nearly incoherent. I asked him if he would show me the formula he uses to access these "high angelic beings." He agreed and gave me the code. I did the same process and sure enough, there they were, ready to give their usual scrambled messages. When I asked them who they were, they admitted to being lower astral plane beings who just wanted to "help" my friend. When presented with this information, my friend said he did not care. He did not want to seek more reliable spirit sources, as he was making a lot of money just doing what he was doing. It is important to look at people's motivations.

To channel some well-known person from the past is such a popular thing to do now, just as it was popular a few years ago to recall a past life as an Egyptian pharaoh or as one of Jesus' disciples. It is vital to be discriminating when a friend says she just began channeling last week and she is the voice for St. Germain. She could be tapping into the energy of that master, to be sure, but when channelers begin throwing out many names of well-known entities or historical figures they are channeling, I become skeptical. Often such a situation is based on ego; they are hoping to receive the attention or recognition they do not get in other aspects of their lives.

The situation is completely different when someone begins to channel a being he has never heard of and only later discovers who the entity is and in what area of specialty that being serves. The best source a person can contact for channeling is his own higher self or oversoul. That way he knows he is accessing information for his highest purposes and is receiving that which is true for himself, for ego is no longer in the way.

The Business of Ascension

It is important to realize that no one ascends simply because he or she desires to or has paid someone for an initiation into Ascension. Many problems that exist on Earth at the present time are due to the misuse of power. If everyone who wanted to be an ascended master could simply will it to be so, those who have not yet learned to control their egos would greatly endanger Earth's survival.

Ascension has become a big business. There are many individuals traveling around the world teaching classes on ascension, which is good. Others are claiming to be ascended masters and are performing ascension initiations, which is not so good. If a person says that for a certain sum of money he or she can move someone up thirty levels, the question must be, "thirty levels of what?" After attending an initiation, participants must ask themselves what they can do that they could not have done before they spent the money. Any hesitation about attending a weekend workshop should be resolved by requesting to attend the Friday night session for a nominal fee before making a decision about attending the next two days; most presenters will agree to that.

There are more and more people traveling the circuit and promising great accomplishments to those who attend their workshops. It is important to recognize the truth or falsity of their claims. If someone says they are ascended, the following list of characteristics for ascended masters will help in determining the validity of that statement.

1. They are *never* concerned about the future.

2. They are *always* nonjudgmental.

3. They *always* love unconditionally.

4. They are *never* tired and, in fact, do not need to sleep.

5. They do not require food, but were they to eat or drink in celebration, they would consume only natural foods.

6. They *never* get spacey or ungrounded or lose their focus. Some of the more dramatic presenters equate being ungrounded with becoming fifth-dimensional, but nothing could be further from the truth. Humans are here to balance their energies with those of the Earth Mother.

7. They appear radiant and much younger than their years, for they have stopped aging.

8. They *never* accept money, for they can manifest all their needs.

9. They *never* need to read or study because they access universal

information.

10. They can become fourth- or fifth-dimensional and invisible to most people.
11. They do not claim to be able to make anyone an ascended master by performing an initiation. Everyone must earn his or her own mastery, and it is not possible to exchange money for ascension.
12. They *never* need to say they are ascended; it is apparent.

Personal Integration

Physically and etherically the process of ascension will mean the diminishing of aches and pains. For example, flu and cold symptoms will last for a shorter time. Headaches will stop before they are fully developed. Symmetry and ease of movement will return to the body. There will be a transformation of the dense, physically imperfect body into a radiantly beautiful Light-filled form that is translucent. As sensitivity increases, emanations of Light will radiate from various organs and systems in the body. Along with seeing the colors of those beams, it will be possible to hear their celestial tones as well.

Emotionally, humans are learning to be in total control of their feelings. This ability will manifest initially as an absence of all fear. (Metaphysicians say there would be no illness if there were no fear. The joy a person experiences in every moment will carry over into his surroundings and others will be drawn in. I have experimented many times by entering a small store when there were no customers present and counting the minutes until it became crowded. On a subconscious level people want to be near a peace-filled aura. Anyone can try this. It is also possible to recall circumstances in which there was plenty of space around but other individuals chose to stand or sit in very close proximity.

Mentally, ascension will mean a leap forward in consciousness. At the moment most people's subconscious minds are fighting with their normal or waking conscious minds and people are, for the most part, oblivious to their superconscious minds. When all thinking is con-sciously under the direction of the higher self, a person quickly evolves and is able to observe how rapidly it is possible to create whatever is truly needed in life. Everyone is becoming a creator.

As all three areas — physical/etheric, emotional and mental — come into harmony, people will no longer be negatively affected by anything or anyone. They will be able to make all spaces their own spaces, and their experiences will be the best that are possible. Personal growth will keep pace with planetary growth. Each person will shine forth to all human-ity, not alone but connected, Light to Light, with all others at his or her vibrational frequency.

In summary, it is time to start letting go of the material world, remembering that it is an illusion, and to spend more time in meditation and even in daydreaming, because they both access other planes. Work-ing with dreams is important, for by going within, it is possible for a per-son to learn who he is and to understand his connection to the Creator. It is also vital for a person to practice dominion over his thoughts and emotions, for he is creating his reality, moment by moment. Trusting in the perfect timing of all events and desires in life is essential, as is learn-ing to recognize synchronistic events and take advantage of them.

Humans must learn to have patience with themselves and love the bodies they have chosen . . . love them into perfection.

Notes

1. This means that the resurrected body vibrates faster than the third-dimen-sional body, giving it a shimmering appearance.

The Millennium

Arise, shine: for thy light is come.

Isaiah 60:1

There will come a moment when the old shell, or vibration, of Earth will fall away. It will be consumed by the glorious energies of peace, Light and love. As Earth resurrects in that "twinkling of an eye," her new and awesome magnificence will influence every other planet in this solar system, every star in this universe and all of creation itself, for as each lesser being ascends, all above are able to move forward. The lesser have restricted the greater, but that will no longer be true. Sufficient numbers of people have grown individually and now the whole is affected. This movement is cyclical and past cycles have led humanity to where it is at present.

History of the Seasons

Just as Earth experiences the seasons of each year, so has the collective of humankind experienced its seasons. These seasons and ages overlap and penetrate one another in the chaos of beginnings. Every aspect of creation throughout the universe moves in ever-expanding spirals. Individual life, planetary life, galactic life, even universal life slowly progresses ever farther, ever outward until that time when it turns in upon itself.

The ancient wisdom teaches that Earth also experiences the grand seasons in her evolution. Her cycles begin with the coming of spring, a glorious time when civilization begins to send forth deep roots which penetrate the Earth and green shoots which stretch out above the soil. The strength and vigor are nearly unstoppable as all of the nature kingdoms send out their greatest efforts. Humanity is aware of this and is eager to cooperate. It is the period of greatest visible movement and acceptance. The master teachers shower their inspirational wisdom upon all who will listen. Those teachings are anchored in human hearts. This period can last for thousands of years, as it did during the time of Lemuria and Atlantis. Humanity continued to progress rapidly in every area because of willingness to accept Divine Guidance.

Then the second great cycle of summer arrives. This period is evidenced by the outward expression of culture. The arts, philosophy and theology expand. However, only a fraction of the knowledge handed down by the masters has germinated. That which has been integrated or brought to fruition makes a tremendous difference in the lives and minds of the people. Architecture, literature and even fashion are affected, and they expand to beautify everyone's world. Diversity is the result of creativity during this cycle. Separation occurs among cultures as each develops its uniqueness. The excellence of individual races becomes evident. Even spirituality becomes divergent. This period allows humanity to further develop its concepts of God. It was evidenced by the flowering of culture and spirituality as civilization spread from Atlantis to Europe, the Middle East, the Far East and the Americas.

Then the planet moves into autumn and the creative force begins to slow. The energy that had worked to expand humans beyond their previous limitations has waned. People are no longer stimulated to develop their maximum potential. An example of this is the inspirational Greek civilization which eventually succumbed to a preoccupation with the material world. During this cycle, the creative genius goes beyond simple, clear beauty and tends to produce excesses such as the rococo style of architecture as it evolved in eighteenth century Europe. The earlier cycle produced large temples with simple interiors where initiates could concentrate on spiritual teachings. Unlike those built during the summer cycle, churches built during the autumn period increase in number and become excessively grand and ornate so as to detract people from their original spiritual purpose. The church in Rome became the ultimate example of extravagance. Creativity during that period moved past the stage of inspired originality and into unrestrained extravagance. It is similar to the nature kingdoms' giving forth one last effort, but that last exertion never matches the quality of the earlier fruits. Thus, the leaves of the tree begin to wither and fall. People watch what is happening but believe they are powerless to change the nature of the cycle.

Humanity seems to hibernate during the cold, dark season of evolution. Then there is no spiritual growth. The icy winter cycle plunges the masses into an age of ignorance. It is a time of despair and separation that causes the individual ego to grow out of proportion as it greedily imagines a need for power and the accumulation of material wealth for survival.

With only a few exceptions the human link to divine inspiration is lost during this cycle. Without a link to wisdom, truth becomes superstition, and superstition breeds fear. Priceless texts containing the wisdom of the ages are lost due to deliberate destruction or are hidden until a later time. For example, in ancient times the library at Alexandria was ravaged, and, more recently, the Chinese have tried to destroy the ancient manuscripts in Tibet.

Black magic appears and the connection to the lower astral plane becomes stronger. That is followed by witch hunts and ritualistic murders of anyone accused of crimes involving previously acquired spiritual gifts. It is during these dark ages that master teachers appear. They try to awaken humanity from its obsession with separatism, prejudice, hatred and greed. Those who are fearful of the teachers' influence arrange to have them burned, crucified or murdered in some way.

In spite of the darkness, there have always been evolved beings who have come into physical bodies to inspire humanity, reminding people of their potential. They have had to hide their Light by speaking in metaphors and teaching with symbols, but nonetheless humans have been inspired by the Freemasons, the Rosicrucians, the Knights of the Holy Grail and the alchemists. Lives have been transformed by the words of Shakespeare, and the genius of Leonardo da Vinci, Wagner and Beethoven, as well as by spiritual leaders. Their individual sparks of Light have made a difference during the winter cycle. While most of humanity, on the surface, appears to be dormant, there is still growth occurring deep within. Earth is now reaching the end of this long winter cycle of darkness, and great stirrings are being felt throughout the planet.

The first rays of the Age of Aquarius became visible two hundred years ago. The dawning was marked by those who brought to the world a new science through spirituality. Such men as Emanuel Swedenborg, Isaac Newton and Nikola Tesla experimented tirelessly. The birth of the Spiritualist movement in the middle of the nineteenth century brought religion, science and the occult together. Madam Blavatsky, Mary Baker Eddy and Alice Bailey became influential and recognizable forces for progress.

The inspiration of these people heralded a relatively short spring season as humanity quickly progressed through the last layers of the third dimension. Now humanity stands at the brink of a productive summer cycle which ushers in the Golden Age and the transition into the fifth dimension. One age does not end abruptly and another suddenly begin. The ages are intricately woven, just as time and space have made up the warp and woof of the fabric of human lives. During the winter period, a thread of genius can rise colorfully to the surface and then slowly submerge again. There are areas on this planet that are still locked in darkness and seeming stagnation of the winter cycle, while other regions are fully in the experience of spring.

The greatest evidence of this is that the dire predictions from the past are being revised. There is no longer talk of a third world war to annihilate nearly all of the population so that Earth would have to begin again from the crudest stages. There is greater awareness on the part of average citizens regarding the use of control by self-serving organizations, big business and the government. Humanity is beginning to awaken. The numbers of people striving for enlightenment are growing phenomenally. They are affecting the collective unconscious in many areas.

This awakening makes people aware that they are sparks of the Divine, even though they had felt for so long that their sparks were powerless. It is now the season when the sparks accelerate, adding tremendous energy to each individual's full potential. There is a steadily growing realization among people that they have never been alone — never! Suddenly there is no longer just individual divine power, but there is now collective divine power.

How Humans Relate to Earth

The mistake people make is that they want to change the planet. They want to stop deforestation, stop the pollution affecting the atmosphere and the water supplies, and stop inhumane treatment of animals, along with many other issues. They argue among themselves in their various groups about the best way to accomplish these goals. What they have forgotten is that Earthly perfection can be patterned only upon individual perfection, and to arrive at human perfection, it is necessary to look at the self as an organism similar to the planet.

Earth's oceans, rivers and streams correspond to the emotional body of the human being. That means emotions affect everything in the body that is fluid, especially the glands and lymphatic system. Negative emotions are highly contagious. As a person evolves, he or she becomes more focused, and eventually, the power of a single individual's negative emotions could kill someone. It has been said that two minutes of anger poison the human system for up to nine months. Anger produces a chemical that compromises the immune system, and it creates sediment that clogs the normal flow of emotions. Feelings of resentment are said to be a common factor in cancer patients. Scientists have now isolated a chemical produced by laughter which is being administered to cancer patients at $40,000 per treatment. Negative emotions also cause confusion and distortion of incoming information, while positive emotions promote healing and inner peace.

The atmosphere of Earth relates to the mental body. Clouds of pollution dim the ability to think clearly and use logic. Mental confusion is played out in the thunder and lightning of atmospheric storms. Sometimes the mind reacts like a tornado, whirling around and around; at such a time, it is impossible to concentrate. During other periods, the mind drives on relentlessly with the force of a hurricane, no longer being rational but operating out of an irrational sense of purpose. Becoming aware of the mind's thoughts and controlling them is one of the quickest paths to ascension.

The physical land masses of Earth relate to the physical body. As long as a person's body is ill or in pain, that sensation will be carried into the Earth Mother. The diseased bodies of those who died of illness and are buried in the ground continue to negatively affect Earth. Some of the poisons ingested by humans are from crop pesticides which also contaminate the soil. So it is clear that the problem is circular.

Wars have devastating effects on the planet. It is not difficult to understand that wars affect the emotional, mental and physical bodies of humans; therefore, Earth's body must also suffer. There are numerous

A TECHNIQUE FOR SELF-HEALING

One way to feel wonderful is to maintain a synchronized beat among the emotional, mental and etheric bodies. To be effective and rejuvenating, the beats must key off the heart. Most importantly, the pulse of the human heart should synchronize with the pulse of Earth. Healers naturally attune to 7.83 Hertz, which means they are vibrating at the same frequency as Earth.

Begin by relaxing completely and concentrating on slow rhythmic breathing. Next, consciously slow your heart until it is no longer beating in rhythm with the stress all around you. Sense the rhythmic beat of your Earth Mother's heart. It is easier to do this if you are sitting on a large rock or lying in the grass or on a sandy beach. Slow all your bodily rhythms until you become the rock or the land or the ocean.

Now form yourself into a fluffy cloud. You have no density at all. Birds fly through you. Travel around the world in your cloud body. Bring that feeling back into your physical body. Make your physical self as light as possible.

Visualize your body passing through flowers, walls, trees. Nothing can stop you because you are so light. Travel anywhere you wish and experience other forms. You can even travel deep into space in your Light body. When you are ready to come back, just become aware of all your organs and systems again. Slowly open your eyes and smile.

One of the causes of jet lag is being separated from Earth for long periods of time. I have been living out of a suitcase for several years, and I have noticed the aging effects of being airborne during lengthy overseas flights. Now I wear a small Micro Harmonizer from Livewave Electronics, Ltd., when I fly. It pulses the Earth energy cycles to my body and greatly reduces jet lag. If you travel frequently, maintain your connection to Earth.

small wars going on at this time.

Until every human learns to purify his inner space, it will be impossible to heal the planet. Many times, people who protest against various issues love to protest. Often, when one issue is resolved, they search for another battle to fight because they have a strong need to work outside themselves; but they do not have the courage to look within and see what their own problems are.

Humans Are Spirits with Bodies

It is extremely important now that all humans consciously remember that they are spirits that have bodies. Never speak of those bodies in any way that is less than positive. It is vital to remember that the brain believes everything its owner says or thinks and it then creates that reality.

People can no longer afford to gossip or speak negatively of others. What they do not like about others is always a reflection of what they do not like about themselves. A person who dislikes someone for being a sloppy housekeeper and keeps his or her own house immaculate, might assume this rule of reflection does not always apply, but there is sure to be an untidy aspect somewhere. It might be a cluttered mind, a closet or an area other people do not see but which exists nonetheless.

Words of criticism or condemnation feed those who live on bitterness and hatred. It is good to speak the truth but also to realize that truth is little more than an opinion on the third-dimensional plane. People create "truth" to reinforce their beliefs about reality. Truths are pictures drawn in the mind; it is wise to keep that mind open, yet discerning.

Discernment is another key for living through the ascension process. It is an aid in getting past judgment and ego. By using other senses, it is easier for a person to evaluate what is truth for himself or herself while acknowledging it might not be truth for others.

Some New Age publications have so many conflicting stories in one issue that a reader could become very confused. That is where discernment comes in. It is important to take in the information that resonates personally and either discard the rest or, preferably, put it on a mental shelf until later; many concepts must await their proper moment.

Once a person has become aware of his "I am" statements and his gossip (which is always detrimental to someone else and makes the speaker feel superior) and has learned discernment, he can then begin paying attention to his thoughts. The most important idea to remember is that it is impossible to worry when focused in the moment! Scientific tests have revealed how much of the body's energy is expended through thought, and it was learned that worry uses up energy reserves much more quickly than any other kind of thought. It is far better to focus on uplifting words such as beauty, joy, peace, harmony, angels and love.

Lessons of Love

At this time, all of life is about learning the lessons of love. The sooner humans learn them, the more quickly they can move into the fifth dimension. These critical lessons include taking responsibility, identifying what is of value in life and understanding that there are no victims and no accidents. If life seems to be more difficult than ever, it is because many people have asked to learn their lessons as quickly as possible so that they might be finished with them. But they will never learn their lessons if they blame someone else for creating the problems in their lives. People give themselves one test after another until they are sure they have mastered a given situation. Everyone chooses to be in the right place at the right time with exactly the right people who will help them learn a particular lesson.

Everything is either love or a lesson in love.

As multidimensional beings people are now tapping into the lessons of others to round out their own experiences. Some strange characters might turn up, but they are appearing to trigger old memories. Everything is moving at lightning speed and therefore encounters are also happening that way. Aspects of mother, brother, teacher, minister, priest or friend might appear in anyone an individual encounters in order to help point out that we are all one. This is similar to a final exam people are giving themselves so they can graduate from this limited physical reality. As humans step fully into the next dimension, they must have the clear perception and understanding that they are capable of recognizing the illusions of this reality. Then they can help to awaken others who are ready.

Humans as Creators

It is imperative that people understand that they are creating their lives moment by moment. They should be making it is as loving and perfect and protected as they can imagine it to be. The more people become convinced that their divine selves are their true selves, the more they move into perfection. At that point it is no longer necessary for them to surround themselves with white Light, for they are Light! The higher their vibration, the more Light they reflect outward. Any person who attempts to harm them, even through negative thoughts, has his own negativity reflected back to him instantly.

The higher a person's level of vibration, the more intricate or intense are the lessons he has chosen to learn. But one day he will awaken and find that he has grown beyond the lessons of illusion. It no longer matters who is doing what to whom, and he can no longer be pulled into any confrontation. He simply steps back and observes. That becomes very frustrating for all those who have manipulated him into being a part of their problems in the past. They will then try even harder to involve him. Instead, he showers them with love and nonjudgment. His mind then moves beyond belief in cause and effect, which comes from left-brained rationality, for he can see beyond duality. Each day he experiences greater love for the perpetrator of a crime as well as for the victim.

The greatest truths of all the ages are becoming his to live.

Another interesting aspect of ascension is that eventually a point is reached when it is no longer necessary to forgive. Once a person stops judging, he realizes that no one has ever harmed anyone intentionally. People act out of the fear in which they were programmed early in life and can only behave in the way they have been conditioned to respond. When the person working on ascension reaches this stage, he then begins to witness life from a detached perspective. Holding no judgment against someone means there is nothing to forgive. When this stage is achieved, many of the daily hassles disappear, and nothing really matters except existing in unconditional love.

The last subject to mention is the joy that comes from living life free from illusionary beliefs. A natural high accompanies the freedom of knowing that it is no longer necessary to be responsible for solving everyone else's problems. Without worry, it is possible to become lost in the beauty of a sunset, to reflect the radiance of a baby's smile or experience deep joy for no special reason. Suddenly, the person without illusions realizes he can change the energy in a group meeting or a shopping mall simply by means of his loving presence. As he learns to use his new abilities, he begins to understand how much he can accomplish together with other Lightworkers.

When the term "Lightworkers" first came into vogue, people thought they were working "in the Light." As true as that statement might be, world-servers, by the nature of their self-sacrifice, are actually becoming more Light. They are a part of a very special team that came here to help the planet and everything connected with her. It is wise for Lightworkers to surround themselves with others who think and feel as they do, for through group sharing and meditation, Light energy increases exponentially. It is now time for people to create the situations they desire to exist on Earth through their visualizations and energies directed in a powerful manner. No longer will people look up to any other human as a guru or teacher. Each must recognize his own divine spirit and call upon his own higher self for guidance and also upon the many angels who are here in service at this time. Each person must learn to see perfection in everything — and so it will be. People are rising into higher vibrations as each day passes. As they grow in perfection — not only their own perfection but the perfection they see in others — that energy is directly reflected into the planet. That will create the millennium all are longing for. Peace in the heart creates peace on Earth.

Earth Ascension

The Great Spiritual Being who ensouls the Earth Mother is shedding her dense shell with all its imperfections. In its place will be a most radiant mantle of Light emanations. Her new grid lines are already blazing with crystalline energy as she aligns with a new pole star. Earth will stabilize once again. The rays of all the guiding planets will flow directly into each area of the world, as required. A bubble of Christed energy will slowly create a new atmosphere and under that sparkling canopy there will be no violent storms, no wrathful winds or devastating earthquakes. Everything within the loving embrace of Mother Earth will be tenderly and lovingly cared for.

Magnificent etheric geometric Cities of Light will once again radiate their brilliance. Many will be constructed with walls made entirely from rays of Light. The process of building them will entail cooperation with the living intelligence of the elements. Structures can then be fashioned by thought. Translucent temples will again shine in the sun and be used as they were originally intended. One of the purposes will be to communicate with the Higher Intelligences.

Gold will be recognized for its beauty as ornamentation, never again to be used financially. Nothing will be owned. Everything will be shared for the benefit of all. There will be no need for doors or locks and keys; hearts and homes will be open. Even Earth herself will be open.

She will be one of the most frequently visited sites in the universe. Travel will be easier then because Earth is moving from her position at the distant edge of the galaxy to a new location much closer to the Great Central Sun as a direct result of her greatly intensified vibration. Earth will be recognized for the successful experiment in duality and density that has led her to unparalleled splendor.

From Human to Godman

And humans . . . what magnificence they will project! Like rainbows in the sky, they will reflect the new Light spectrum, one that contains a more extensive array of hues than the physical eye can now perceive. Each evolved organ will sound its particular note. Each of the bodies which are a part of one soul will have its own song. As a human moves and interacts with all aspects of the self, he or she becomes a symphony of light and sound that remembers its connection to its higher self, its oversoul group and its holographic self.

There will be joyous reunions as many who worked on the Earth plane over the eons of time are reunited by the thousands. So much knowledge will have been garnered from Earth's experiment that everyone will have an intense interest in helping other worlds where such experiments are still in progress. The celebration will last a thousand years, and during that time Earth will become lighter and brighter. She will no longer appear as a blue marble but rather as topaz, amethyst, emerald and diamond; sparkling, shining so brilliantly that physical eyes would not be able to gaze at her directly.

Humans will move on to future realities but will long to return from time to time. All the universe will continue to value the experimentation that was carried out on the radiant little blue planet at the edge of the galaxy. In spite of the many beings which make up each human, the beings that are here now have played the most unique and invaluable role in helping to free Mother Earth from the third dimension and birth into the fifth dimension. These special individuals will always be remembered with deepest respect from those existing in every dimension.

All the angels from the Heavenly realms that surround and penetrate Earth salute humans with their music of the spheres and send their loving appreciation.

Joy!

Love!

Namaste!

APPENDIX

Video Tape

BIOGETIC HOLOPHASING
Lightworks Audio & Video
P.O. Box 665193
Los Angeles, CA 90066-4507

Learn advanced methods of healing and working with life-force energy in this practical and well-illustrated video. It is divided into four sections for ease of viewing:
- a graphically illustrated history with an explanation of the electromagnetic fields of the body
- information on how healing works,
- the BioGetic Holophasing process is demonstrated on a client
- a powerful guided meditation.

(also available in PAL versions in German and English)
"Nancy Clark, Ph.D., demonstrates her healing methods and how they help people heal illness and release past lives and genetic programming. Clark has a knack for explaining what she does with crystal-clear simplicity." Conscious Choice Magazine.

Audio Tape Series
Lightworks Audio & Video
Phone: 1-800-795-TAPE

Journeys of Remembrance

A series of meditation tapes has been designed to reawaken past and future memories so the individual might move forward in the light as quickly as possible. These guided visualizations are accompanied by beautiful music which leads you gently into the Alpha state.

Atlantis & Lemuria

Travel back in time and see life as it was. Visit the Temple of the Dolphins for healing on your visit to Atlantis and the Temple of Wisdom in Lemuria. This tape is designed to help you remember your lifetimes on these continents.

Access the Light Body

This experience is for anyone interested in the Ascension of the physical body into the Fifth-Dimensional Body of Light. The first side is an explanation of the different dimensions and the future of the physical body. Side two offers a trip into the future of Earth after you have learned how to put on your "garment of light." You will have the opportunity to meet the Cosmic Christ.

Discover Your Angels

You will journey deep into space to the site of the Crystal Palace. There, among the thousands gathered, you will meet your special angel who guides you now. The second side offers a magical journey over the rainbow bridge. Waiting for you is your angel to teach you techniques for self-love as well as for creating greater peace for you and the planet.

A boxed, two-cassette series based on the book, *World In Ascension*, will be available in the fall of 1995.

A TREASURY OF ADDITIONAL READING

Chapter 1   THE FALL OF CAMELOT

Ancient Astronauts, Cosmic Collisions and Other Popular Theories About Man's Past, William H. Stiebing, Jr.

Genesis Revisited (and all other books by this author), Zecharia Sitchin

Pyramid Odyssey, William R. Fix

Pyramid Prophecies, Max Toth

The Gods of Eden, William Bramley

The Orion Mystery, Tobert Bauval and Adrian Gilbert

Up From Eden, A Transpersonal View of Human Evolution, Ken Wilber

Chapter 2   AWAKENING THE INDIVIDUAL

Bridge Of Light, Tools Of Light For Spiritual Transformation, LaUna Huffiness

Don't Think Like a Human!, Kryon

The Gateway of Liberation and *Spiritual Laws: Rules of the Evolutionary Arc*, Mary Gray

Universal Law for the Aquarian Age, Dr. Frank Alper

Chapter 3   A GLOBAL AWAKENING

Earth Spell, The Loss of Consciousness on Earth, Ceanne DeRohan

Serving Planet Earth, John S. Haigh

Shambhala, The Sacred Path of the Warrior, Chogyam Trungpa

The Evolution of Consciousness, Robert Ornstein

The First and Last Freedom, J. Krishnamurti

The Planetary Commission, John Randolph Price

Chapter 4   THE SIGHTING

Earth, Pleiadian Keys to the Living Library, Barbara Marciniak
Revelations of Things to Come, Earlyne Chaney
The Keys of Enoch, J. J. Hurtak
The Year 2000 & After, Torkom Saraydarian

Chapter 5   NEW PERSPECTIVES

Attitudes Toward Other Religions, Owen C. Thomas
Evolution's End, Claiming the Potential of Our Intelligence, Joseph Chilton
  Pearce
Higher Creativity, Liberating the Unconscious for Breakthrough Insights,
  Willis Harman, Ph.D., and Howard Rheingold
Human Possibilities, Stanley Krippner

Chapter 6   ASCENSION/RESURRECTION

Dossier on the Ascension, Serapis Bey
You Are Becoming A Galactic Human, Virginia Essene and Sheldon
  Nidle
Hyperspace, A Scientific Odyssey Through Parallel Universes, Time Warps,
  and the 10th Dimension, Michio Kaku
Initiation, Human and Solar, Alice A. Bailey
The Astonishing Hypothesis, The Scientific Search for the Soul, Francis
  Crick

Chapter 7   THE MILLENNIUM

Apocalypse Now, The Challenges of Our Times, Peter Roche de Coppens
Bridging Science and Spirit, Norman Friedman
The Only Planet of Choice, Essential Briefings from Deep Space, Phyllis V.
  Schlemmer & Palden Jenkins
The Way of the Essenes, Christ's Hidden Life Remembered, Anne and
  Daniel Meurois-Giaudan

ABOUT THE AUTHOR

Nancy Clark is a dedicated world-server. She travels to many countries, teaching various subjects, but her two favorites are "Ascension" and "BioGetic Holophasing." She had not consciously thought about the subject of ascension until nearly six years ago. At that time, a woman approached her during a conference they were both attending. The woman handed Nancy her card and said, "I know that I am not going to die in this lifetime. My guides have instructed me to come to this conference and meet the person who would guide me in this process. You are that person. Call me when you are ready to teach ascension." Somewhat surprised, Nancy accepted the card and the woman disappeared.

Throughout the following year, small bits of information on ascension kept coming to her. Exactly one year later, Nancy taught her first course in "Ascension." The original group, plus participants of later classes, have continued to meet monthly since that time. By following the ups and downs in the lives of the participants over the years, she has had an excellent resource for information regarding the process involved in ascension. Nancy has had to readjust her teachings many times to adapt them to her own expanding consciousness. The most amazing discovery has been the number of people around the world who do not understand the meaning or implications of the word and yet are "triggered" by ascension and feel they must attend the workshop.

Another area of interest is healing. Nancy's guides would not permit her to learn any healing modalities such as Reiki and Jin Shin Juitsu until she had evolved her own techniques. She was working with the electromagnetic field of the body long before it was so popular. Her method of BioGetic Holophasing works with the lower bodies, clearing them, heightening their vibrations and putting them in perfect alignment. It is then possible to take the electrical "shells" of past lives and phase them through the high-energy fields of the present bodies. This procedure clears past-life trauma or weakness which may be affecting the present physical body. This fast simple method clears and heals without all the side effects of past life pain; emotional or mental.

For several years Nancy has been involved in a project to reduce stress in post-communist countries. Her colleague is a doctor of psychology in the Czech Republic. They have presented their findings at the European Professional Psychologists Association.

Nancy has also lectured at the United Nations on the subject, "The Path to World Ascension." She has given up her regular practice as a psychotherapist but is able to counsel many people in the course of her world travels. She has discovered a reason for optimism, because every country is experiencing an awakening. Wonderful humans everywhere are working to change themselves and the planet. They have filled Nancy with optimism and a shared belief in a glorious future for the Earth Mother.